"We all live in a frantic and hecti[c] [...]
directed rest, people can suffer [...]
could alter your life and lifestyle. [...]

—**Mrs. Heather Olford**, wife of the late Dr. Stephen Olford

"If you are like me (and a million other women in the world today), one of your most frequent responses to 'How are you?' is . . . '*I'm tired!*' In her new book, Denise George tackles an issue that is crucial in the lives of contemporary women everywhere: the need for rest! Based solidly on the Scriptures and personalized through real-life experiences we can all relate to, Denise leads us on a journey to discover fourteen specific types of biblical rest that is sure to impact every reader's life. You'll find practical tools to use in your private devotional time as well as helps for interactive group study. This book is a must-read for every woman whose heart sighs for a respite from the frenetic pace of daily living in today's world."

—**Diane M. Fink**, Director, Aglow Institute of Ministry (AIM)

"Imagine, if you can, *rest*. I wish my wife Rebecca and I would have read this book early in our marriage. Throughout the years, both of us have needed more rest, and, if we had done so, would have accomplished more. This book is filled with Scripture and pages of practical suggestions on how busy women can rest, not just physically, but more importantly, to find an inner rest that gives strength and focus to the soul. Do yourself a favor and read this book, then pass it along to a friend who also needs to be assured that there is hope for the weary."

—**Dr. Erwin and Rebecca Lutzer**, The Moody Church, Chicago

"Denise George has provided an invaluable resource for Christian women in *A Woman's Right to Rest*! With ever increasing demands on their time and energy, women need to hear that they have a biblical mandate to rest. Denise's book is a very beneficial biblical permission slip to take some well-deserved time of rest."

—**Richard Land**, President, Southern Baptist's Ethics & Religious Liberty Commission

"This book is a must read for all women who are worn down by lifestyles so hectic that they have abandoned their spiritual being. This easy-to-read book gives us spiritual guidance, helping us become better able to cope as we go about our daily living. It puts us back in touch with our spiritual side thereby allowing us to experience a more calm and peaceful state of mind. It reminds us of how God is truly there for us in all we do; we only need to be still and listen."

—**Judge Helen Shores Lee**, co-author of *The Gentle Giant on Dynamite Hill*

"In this most readable volume, Denise George has once again offered strength, wisdom, and insight for her readers. Grounded in Scripture, illustratively shaped by her own experiences and those of others, *A Woman's Right to Rest* provides thoughtful and wise guidance worthy of serious reflection by women (and men) of all ages."

—**David and Lanese Dockery**, President and First Lady, Union University

"In music, 'rest' means 'to pause'—and all of us need to learn (as musicians already know) the value of pausing. Christian women in their busy, multi-tasking, demanding lives can benefit from the remarkable insights of Denise George. Remember, at times, the most spiritual action you can take is simply to 'take a nap'—to rest as Elijah did in 1 Kings 19. As a wife, mother, author, and lecturer, Denise George knows what it is to 'be busy'—and thus how important 'rest' becomes. Wholeheartedly (as her former pastor), I encourage you to 'make time to rest'—and as you do, enjoy reading this book!"

—**Charles T. Carter**, pastor

"Denise George has written numerous important books, but this volume stands out among her other works because of the urgency of the message. As parents, grandparents, authors, and active church members for decades, we can testify to the significance of *A Woman's Right to Rest*. Pressures on women in the home, church, and marketplace have become too weighty to ignore. Denise George's brilliant and timely book not only warns us of the problem, it provides biblical and practical advice on how we can begin to reverse a destructive trend. Men, as well as women, need to read this book."

—**Lyle and Mary Dorsett**, co-pastors of Christ the King Anglican Church, Birmingham, Alabama

"Whether martyrs in the arena, managers of estates, or the rock centers of the family, an honored convoy of Christian women down the years has continued to tread the highroads of service—sometimes to the point of exhaustion. This latest book by Denise George will help us all—both women and their men—to take in what the Bible promises us, at this the most restless period in living memory."

—**Richard Bewes, OBE**, author; former Rector of All Souls Church, Langham Place, London, England

"Make an appointment to read *A Woman's Right to Rest*. It will be like visiting your doctor's office. Join the other patients who are in need of the Divine Physician's care. Enter His presence, share your symptoms, receive His compassionate diagnosis, prognosis, and prescription to rest in Him. But, you must follow His personal instructions, penned by Denise George, that are therapeutic for mind, body, and soul.

Keep your appointment with the Divine Physician, penned through the words of this profound, practical, and personal author. Your life will not be the same. Don't cancel the appointment. There is holistic healing for you and all women."

—**Sheila Bailey**, Sheila B Ministries, Inc.

"All Christians should have a 'sabbatical identity.' In this prophetic book, Denise George indicates why women—especially mothers—are vulnerable to forfeit this covenantal blessing. Instead, 'busyness' becomes our 'Egyptian bondage.' This practical book is a great awakening to living 'in Christ.'"

—**James M. Houston**, Professor of Spiritual Theology, Regent College, Vancouver, B.C., Canada

A
WOMAN'S
RIGHT
TO REST

A WOMAN'S RIGHT TO REST

14 Types of Biblical Rest That Will Transform Your Life

Denise George

LEAFWOOD
PUBLISHERS

A WOMAN'S RIGHT TO REST
14 Types of Biblical Rest That Will Transform Your Life

LEAFWOOD
PUBLISHERS

LIBRARY OF CONGRESS CATALOGING-IN-PUBLICATION DATA
George, Denise.
A woman's right to rest : 14 types of biblical rest that will transform your life / Denise George.
   p. cm.
Includes bibliographical references and index.
ISBN 978–0-915547–87-6 (alk. paper)
1. Christian women--Religious life. 2. Rest--Biblical teaching. I. Title.
BV4527.G45725 2012
248.8'43--dc23

                                                2012016231

Cover design by Thinkpen Design, LLC
Interior text design by Sandy Armstrong

Leafwood Publishers is an imprint of
Abilene Christian University Press
1626 Campus Court
Abilene, Texas 79601

1–877-816–4455
www.leafwoodpublishers.com

In loving memory of my beautiful friend,
Ann Williamson.

With thanksgiving for her life, her love, her wisdom,
and the dear friendship of her two children
—Robin Skipper and Becky Carlisle.

TABLE OF CONTENTS

ACKNOWLEDGMENTS

My gratitude to Leafwood Publishers for publishing this book—Gary Myers, Leonard Allen, Robyn Burwell—and for my book agent, Greg Johnson, who provided guidance and contracts. Thank you Beeson Divinity School faculty, staff, and students for many reasons over my many years of writing books. My family deserves my deepest gratitude, especially my husband, Dr. Timothy George, founding Dean of Beeson Divinity School, Samford University. I want to thank all the wonderful women who shared their personal stories with me. I want to say a special thank you to all my friends and the members of Boot Camp for Christian Writers who prayed for me as I finished this book, especially Carolyn Tomlin, cofounder of the boot camp and a dear friend.

Foreword

by Dr. Calvin Miller

never tire of Denise George's confessional writing style. I wondered, as I picked up this latest manuscript, if I would feel the same connection her refreshing style automatically communicates. But I felt that all she had to say about women finding their own Sabbath strangely affecting my own view of rest. This book has a rather gender-specific title, but, trust me, there lies within these pages a call to all people, men or women, about how to find your way out of the fatiguing hassle that is not only tiring but destructive.

People who don't rest don't live long, and, even when they do, they degenerate into frowning automatons who grow gray and severe and caustic in their pitiful schedule chasing. They rarely feel pleased with themselves or congratulate themselves on how good they feel. They shortchange their families, trying to "get things done" while all the time "never getting enough done." Then one day they begin to have vague, "unfulfilled" feelings that come from their un-achieving exhaustion. Denise is right. It is time that someone got on God's side and talked about Sabbath rest.

Sabbath rest is one of the Ten Commandments—funny, when you get really busy trying to get things done, you shorten the list. There are only nine commandments. If you run fast enough, long enough, you can just run past God's Word on rest. You're so tired, you collapse in bed, so mad at yourself for not getting more done, you forget God gave us ten commandments.

It always amazes me that the whole idea of rest begins early in Genesis when God takes six days to create the world and then takes one day to rest. Why rest? Does God get tired? No! He rests because, as he puts it on all the others days, "It is good!" He ends each day of creation with a self-affirmation. Does this mean he has created all he might have on days five or six? No, as resplendent as the world is, he might have created more. But he rests because "God saw that it was good!" The same is true for us: a job well done doesn't mean that we couldn't have done more but that all that we did was well done. So we rest.

Denise George wants you to live with a sense of completion so that you don't find your Sabbaths pasted together with "I sure wish I had done more!" Denise is a fun person: she laughs wholeheartedly, and a lunchtime with her always erupts in good times for all, even if she is buying. I suspect that is because she has enough good rest-full down times that she is released to enjoy all times.

In this good work she offers us fourteen key passages from the Bible that outline how to "enter into our rest." Read slowly, or you might miss the argument. If you scan this book, you have missed the whole point of this book. Scanning is a half-way art that is practiced by those most prone to running through their Sabbath at such a pace they have no Sabbaths. It is the severe sin of chopping the Ten Commandments back to nine. So, listen up and slow down.

When the Israelis were making bricks for Pharaoh, he grew disappointed in their output and said to them, "Get back to your burdens" (Exod. 5:4 ESV). Now, of course, we have made such slavery for ourselves. "Get back to your burdens" is the horrible push we put on our own souls. "Why?" asks Denise George. Sabbath is still God's plan. Sabbath, that Hebrew "number seven" says naps are okay. So are "time outs." So are quiet walks. So are fat novels and "sleepy-time tea." So is a crossword puzzle. So are hop-scotch, Monopoly, chick flicks, rose smelling, and a half-dozen psalms, read all at once from an open Bible.

I think my favorite chapter from Denise's book is chapter two, which she bases on Matthew 11:28, "Come to me, all you who are weary and burdened, and I will give you rest." I have loved this passage all my life, but never more than when Pearl Bailey was doing her Black Hello Dolly on Broadway. After every Saturday Night performance, she would come out and sit or stand on the proscenium and take questions from the audience, in a wonderful "talk back" on the play.

One of those nights, someone asked her how she kept so fresh and alive in the role, even after scores and scores of performances. She quoted Matthew 11:28 and said she believed that the hundreds and thousands of weary New Yorkers had paid for the tickets, they came to rest, and that if God gave her the ability to help them rest through watching her sing and waltz her way through a Jerry Herman play, she had served New York well.

This is how I feel about this book.

Denise George is serving a gracious God, who knows how tired and in need of rest you are.

Read and heed and live the fullest life possible.

Rest and live!

Calvin Miller,
Birmingham, Alabama author, preacher, poet, retired professor

INTRODUCTION

My friend, Diane, is a busy wife, mother, homemaker, and freelance writer. Recently I asked her to describe her average day. She responded in this way: "Denise, have you ever seen the clown at the circus that has plates spinning on small, skinny little bamboo poles? He runs around keeping each plate spinning as he adds one more, and then one more, and then one more, until he is running around like a chicken with his head cut off, trying to keep all the plates spinning and not crashing to the floor."

Diane admitted, "That is what my life feels like. I am running around trying to keep up with children, housework, yard work, and entertaining people in my home in an effort to help my husband in his business. The list of responsibilities just continues to grow, and they can be grueling—with no end in sight. I have no choice but to just try to put one foot in front of the other and keep going. Even today, like the clown, I continue to add spinning plates to my day and think 'if I can add just one more thing to my day, or make one more errand—stop on my way somewhere, it will be okay.' I am so exhausted trying to be all things to all people at all times."

How would you describe your average day? Can you identify with Diane? Do you also feel like a frantic circus clown trying to keep numerous plates up in the air spinning on skinny bamboo poles, moving faster and faster to keep them from crashing to the ground and shattering into thousands of pieces? Are you also tired of "trying to be all things to all people at all times"?

If so, you're not alone!

Christian women today are responsible for balancing many different spinning plates. Women, both married and single, are working hard inside and outside their homes, trying to maintain financial balance and pay their medical insurance and electric bills. Married women carry these and additional responsibilities as they try to meet a husband's needs on many fronts—personal, home, and business. Many moms are shouldering these same responsibilities and caring for children. In addition to the overwhelming duties of everyday life, women are working volunteer jobs in their churches and communities, perhaps caretaking for a sick child or elderly parent, and maybe dealing with a multitude of personal issues. It's no wonder that exhaustion has become the new look on the face of today's Christian woman!

Women are tired! Even the men in our churches are beginning to notice our exhaustion. Author John Eldridge writes, "Walk into most churches in America, have a look around, and ask yourself this question: 'What is a Christian woman? ... Don't listen to what is said, look at what you find there. There is no doubt about it. You'd have to admit, a Christian woman is ... tired."[1]

Most Christian women today lead a "spinning plate" life and suffer large amounts of harmful stress brought about by too much work, too many responsibilities, and the unrelenting, and often unrealistic, expectations of others. And they don't seem to be coping with it all very well. Like Diane, they speak of "grueling responsibilities" with "no end in sight."

Recently I asked my busy friend, Lynn, if she ever stopped, sat down, and just rested. Lynn is the wife of a church pastor. She helps him in his church ministry, works a full-time job outside the home, and is rearing two young girls.

She responded, "Denise, the word 'rest' is not in my vocabulary!"

Lynn barely keeps supper on the table and clean clothes in her daughters' closets. As her full-time job responsibilities increase, she wonders how long she can keep up this breakneck pace.

As I look around me, I see a frightening trend growing among Christian women today. They are always multitasking—working, running, moving, and trying to *beat the clock* rushing to meet yet another deadline. For various reasons, these busy women refuse to stop, put their feet up, and rest. What are some of the "reasons"? They say:

- "I don't have time to rest. There's just not enough hours in the day to stop and rest."
- "My family needs more money. How can I rest when I work two jobs?!"
- "I've got too much to do at home and at work. With all these deadlines, I dare not stop. If I do, I won't get everything done!"
- "People depend on me, and if I take time to rest, I might 'let them down.'"
- "I 'feel guilty' when I stop work and rest."
- "Rest? Aren't women supposed to live *sacrificially* for others? Give, give, and then give some more?"
- "Rest is a luxury I can't indulge in right now."
- "My family and friends and fellow church members will think I'm lazy if I spend time resting."
- "I was taught that taking time for oneself and resting is *selfish*."
- "It's not *spiritual* to rest! Women who love the Lord stay busy for him!"
- "I stay super-busy! I'd rather *wear out* than *rust* out!"
- "I know I need to slow down and rest more. But I don't know how."
- "No one ever taught me how to rest. I've always heard that *idleness* is wrong."

- "I try to sleep at least 5 or 6 hours every night. Do I need more rest than that?"
- "My pastor preached on the virtues of the Proverbs 31 woman and told us she should be our example. She worked all the time! Scripture doesn't tell us she ever stopped and 'rested.'"

After years and years of hearing comments like these from Christian women everywhere, I am convinced that women today have not been taught, nor do they understand, the *biblical principles of rest.* They have somehow bought into the false belief that, for the Christian woman, rest is selfish and unscriptural.

Nothing could be further from the truth!

Women today experience many kinds of tiredness. They are not just tired physically but also mentally, emotionally, and spiritually. Women are living hectic lifestyles that are weighing down their bodies, minds, and spirits with harmful and quickly accumulating stress. "What a circus act we women perform every day of our lives," writes Anne Morrow Lindberg.[2]

What happens to a woman's body when she becomes the victim of too much harmful stress over a period of time? Her tired body releases too many stress hormones. These excessive hormones raise her blood pressure, heart rate, and blood sugar level to heights that may lead to multiple health issues, such as depression, anxiety, obesity, abnormal heart beats, acne, and other skin problems.[3]

Over time, high levels of harmful and accumulating stress can rob a woman of her health, and can eventually cause disease and even early death.

In fact, some health professionals link too much harmful stress to the leading causes of human death today: heart disease, strokes, certain cancers, peptic ulcers, insomnia, lung ailments, accidents, cirrhosis of the liver, and other physical ailments.[4]

Frightening trends like these are cultivated by a society that teaches women to "do it all," and "to do it all *perfectly*." Society tells women to climb the corporate career ladder while, at the same time, maintaining a Martha Stewart home, rearing Harvard-bound children, and being the beautiful hour-glass-shaped Cinderella wife whose family lives "happily ever after." Society is pulling women in all different directions all at the same time and expects them to keep a positive attitude, never complain, multitask, and fulfill all their duties with a smile on their face. For a woman to acknowledge a desperate need for rest is not *politically correct* in today's fast-paced, accomplishment-driven society.

Today, even *Christian* women who regularly read and study God's Word from Genesis to Revelation are believing and practicing society's lie. The church itself often teaches and encourages this false philosophy.

Author George Barna believes the problem of tired women in the church is at a critical point and needs immediate attention. He thinks the church may be putting too much work on the shoulders of today's Christian women. He sounds a "note of caution regarding the high price women may pay for carrying excessive levels of spiritual responsibility [in the church]."[5]

Barna urgently advises church pastors to "consider whether or not they are providing sufficient opportunities for women to receive ministry and not just provide ministry to others," and that "we may continue to see tens of thousands of women leaving the church unless there is a widespread, aggressive, thoughtful approach to recognizing and appreciating women."[6]

Barna's suggestion is brilliant, but I see few churches taking his advice. Women are working harder than ever in the increasing number of volunteer jobs in churches. While they may love their time and energy investments in church ministry, these additional jobs can add extra hours and harmful stress to an already overwhelming workload.

I see this "all work, no rest" trend gaining momentum among women in society and in the church. This trend must stop. It is leaving too many tired, overworked women in its destructive path. The time has come to re-examine and re-evaluate the whole concept of rest in the light of God's Word. The results may surprise you!

In *A Woman's Right to Rest*, you'll learn what God's Word says about rest. God, himself, through his Word, gives us—today's Christian women—the right to rest! And he not only grants us divine permission to rest our bodies, minds, emotions, and spirits. He also commands us to rest. Rest is scriptural. Rest is a necessity for Christian women today, not a luxury! Throughout Scripture, in word and example, God encourages us, his daughters, to rest. He even teaches us exactly how to rest.

In my research, I have identified fourteen different, distinctive ways that Scripture encourages us to rest. I have personally practiced these fourteen types of *biblical rest* for years, and they have enhanced and empowered every part of my life. I believe that now is the time to share these life-changing scriptural principles with you.

You can read this book in solitude, learn its wisdom, and practice its suggestions through the "Personal Time to Rest, Study, Reflect, and Pray", or you can get together with friends and share in the "Group Bible Study" section (both located at the end of each chapter).

My prayer is that as you read this book, as you embark upon your life-changing pilgrimage in the area of biblical rest, that God may richly bless you.

Denise George

A Woman's Need for Physical Rest

Come with me by yourselves to a quiet
place and get some rest. (Jesus, Mark 6:31)

ِ *God gives Christian women his*
permission to rest their tired bodies. *ِ*

Tired women need rest! Did you know that Jesus himself gives you and me—today's Christian women—the right to rest?! Our Creator designed our physical bodies to need adequate sleep and regular times of rest. Throughout the pages of this book, I want to introduce you to the many areas of rest God gives his daughters. You may not have ever considered some of these areas of rest. Let's start with a woman's need for physical rest.

As you begin to read this first chapter, may I ask you to do three things? First, brew yourself a cup of calming hot herbal tea and pour it into your favorite china teacup. Second, find a quiet place with a beautiful view where you can be alone and uninterrupted as you read. Third, sit down in a comfortable chair and put your feet up. If you have a favorite dog or cat, place her in your lap or beside your chair, and pet her often. Know that you have just embarked upon the first step of resting your physical body.

THE TWO TYPES OF TIRED

What are the two types of physical "tired"? One is "good tired," the tired we feel after we do a job well or accomplish a difficult task. Our body may feel exhausted, but, after a nap or brief rest, we recover and regain our strength. I experience this type of tired when I work in my garden, especially on hot days, pulling weeds, planting flowers, and watering plants. A cool shower, a glass of cold water, and a fifteen-minute break with my feet up usually restores my energy.

The other physical tired, however, is a "dangerous tired." It can happen when we constantly over-commit our time and energy to others, projects, jobs, committees, and so on and are so burdened with activities and obligations that we cause dis-ease and damage to our bodies. This kind of continual stressful work can deplete our energy, bring on physical fatigue, and even burnout. Some women live life this way, their bodies always struggling with the state of dangerous tired.

I meet women every day who are physically tired and on the verge of burnout, but who, for various reasons, won't stop and rest. Many women won't admit they are tired. They associate confessing exhaustion with complaining or whining. Instead, they keep working and multitasking and often push themselves to sickness in order to keep their secret. At great personal cost, they may continue to carry heavy workloads—at home, at their job, and at church. This unrelieved over-commitment and heavy workload is leading to physically unhealthy women.

One woman recently told me: "I feel so overwhelmed! Surely, God never intended for me to wear so many hats [of responsibility], but yet here I am, wearing them all. Make the world stop spinning. I want to get off!"

Author Henri Nouwen sums up this woman's life (and many others) when he writes, "Our lives often seem like over-packed suitcases bursting at the seams. In fact, we are almost always aware of being behind schedule."[1]

Years ago author Anne Morrow Lindberg compared a woman's busy life to the hub of a wheel. "The problem is not merely one of Woman and Career, Woman and the Home, Woman and Independence," she writes. "It is more basically how to remain whole in the midst of the distractions of life . . . how to remain balanced, no matter what centrifugal forces tend to pull one off center; how to remain strong, no matter what shocks come in at the periphery and tend to crack the hub of the wheel."[2]

Mrs. Lindberg knew that women must constantly multitask, that many people depend on them, and that a woman's life stays full of distractions and interruptions. Remaining balanced and physically strong are major concerns for most women, especially those who continue to experience "shocks at the periphery" that threaten to "crack the hub of the wheel."

How does a Christian woman today remain balanced and strong throughout her busy days? She follows God's plan, woven throughout Scripture, and she learns how to physically rest.

WHAT IS REST?

God gives each one of us the gift of rest. In the physical sense, rest means ceasing work and allowing the body to relax and repair itself. Scripture clearly teaches the value of and need for rest. Women today must tune in to Scripture's teachings about rest and tune out what society tells them about work—climbing the corporate ladder, amassing wealth, and getting ahead at the expense of physical health. Getting enough physical rest will keep a woman whole in the midst of life's work and distractions. God himself gives women permission to rest their bodies. In fact, he encourages it in many varied forms.

During these precious moments, as you sit in your comfortable chair, sip your herbal tea, and read this book, you have stepped away from distractions, those centrifugal forces that tend to pull you off center. You have returned to the source of your renewing strength. You may not realize it yet, but the "cracks in the hub of your wheel" are already beginning to heal. I would advise you to rest your body often in this particular way. God created you to need rest.

Leading a busy life, as most women do these days, doesn't mean becoming a victim of exhaustion. When active women stay alert and respond to the needs of their bodies, they can choose to live balanced lives.

Stop reading for a moment, and place your hand on your heart. Close your eyes, and, for the next few seconds, listen to the beat of your heart. Your heart beats and then it rests. Beats and rests. Beats and rests. Imagine what would happen to your body if your heart beat, beat, beat, and refused to rest. Your heart would soon wear out. It would no longer be able to function the way God created it to function. After each beat, your heart needs a time of rest. God created your entire body to function in this way, dependent upon work and rest and a delicate and necessary balance of both.

GOD RESTED

God himself demonstrates to us the importance of regular rest. Scripture tells us, "By the seventh day God had finished the work he had been doing; so on the seventh day *he rested from all his work.* And God blessed the seventh day and made it holy, because on it he rested from all the work of creating that he had done" (Gen. 2:2–3).

God needs no rest. He has no physical body that tires from his creative work. In resting on the seventh day, our Creator shows us our own need for rest. He sets the example right from the beginning of Scripture, from the very dawn of creation, so we will understand that our physical bodies require rest in order to function and to function well. Rest isn't God's *suggestion* to us but a *mandate* from him since the beginning of time. How can anyone refer to rest as *unscriptural*, or to those who rest as *lazy*? Rest is an important part of God's plan for us as well as for all his creation.

Consider this: the ocean tides reach and then retreat, push forward and then pull back. The year's seasons cause the Earth to grow warm and produce fruits and then grow cold and quiet, allowing the ground to rest between crops. The lily blooms and then withdraws into the soil and rests an entire season before attempting to bloom again. The caterpillar spends time resting in its cocoon before it emerges as a beautifully winged butterfly. Each day divides into light and day, dark and night. Our very bodies respond to the day with work and to the night with sleep. We, too, are creations made to need physical rest after a time of work. God himself by his own example, shows us when and how to rest.

The Necessity of Restful Sleep

In a recent survey, George Barna discovered that "seven out of ten adults (71 percent) . . . look forward 'a lot' to having a refreshing snooze" and that "the fact that tens of millions of Americans dream about having a good night of sleep is indicative of the lifestyle people lead."

Barna notes that "among the most common complaints people have are the struggle to cope with the busyness of their lives, the pressure of family and job responsibilities, and their seemingly unquenchable thirst to be entertained."

He concludes from this study that "we're not busy because somebody makes us busy and stressed; we're that way because we have not learned to say 'no' to appealing opportunities, or to accept the notion that we do not need every experience that's accessible. We voluntarily exhaust ourselves and then wonder why life doesn't seem satisfying. This is one reason why God instituted a day of rest, rather than a day for catching up or gorging on pleasurable activities."[3]

God created our bodies to need restful sleep. Sleep serves as a daily healer. When we sleep, our body rests and restores our energy levels, our muscles begin to relax, our heart rate slows down, and our body temperature decreases. During the deep stages of sleep, our body repairs and regenerates tissues, builds bone and muscle, and strengthens our immune system. Sleep specialists tell us that, as adults, we need seven to eight hours of sleep each day. If we choose to use our nighttime sleep hours to produce work or enjoy entertainment, the next day we can expect impaired thought and memory, depression, and decreased immune response. Lack of necessary sleep also increases our pain perception.[4]

In various stages of life, you, like other women, may experience sleep deprivation. Perhaps your job requires you to work a night shift, and you find it difficult to sleep a full eight hours during daylight hours. Maybe you're a new mother, and your newborn wakes you several times during the night. Worries and problems can often keep women from sleeping. Insomnia or a husband's loud snoring might interfere with a good night's sleep.

Women with sleep disorders need to get help. In multiple ways, sleep deprivation can put you and your family at risk. Imagine a sleep-deprived woman driving with children in her car and trying to negotiate dangerous, heavy traffic. Imagine a woman faced with a crisis and needing to make a life-or-death decision but not having the alertness or mental capacity due to a lack of sleep.

Not only does nighttime sleep renew and repair our tired bodies, but a daily nap helps keep us focused, alert, and physically replenished. Scientists tell us that an afternoon nap will sharpen our senses, increase our waking productivity, and refresh our spirit. They have also discovered that sleep time adds up. "Napping is clearly beneficial to someone who is a normal sleeper but who is getting insufficient sleep at night . . . we don't understand the underlying neurobiology, but sleep time is cumulative."[5]

One recent sleep study showed that people who slept fewer than eight hours a night but took daytime naps proved just as alert as those who slept a full eight hours at night.[6]

If you are not sleeping well at night for whatever reasons, or if you are not getting the recommended eight hours of sleep, make some necessary changes in your life. You may need to see your doctor or undergo a sleep study to rule out medical reasons for your lack of sleep. You may decide to change your sleep habits—invest in a new mattress, sleep in a bedroom alone, go to bed earlier, eliminate nighttime noise in your home, keep your home's temperature cooler, and so on. Whatever you need to do, do it for the sake of your health! Sleep is necessary to your good health! God created you to need adequate sleep.

LISTEN TO YOUR BODY

Learn to rest when your body gets tired. If you listen to your body, your instinctive "rest-nudgers" will call you to remove the multiple plates spinning from their bamboo poles, get away to a quiet place, and rest. Lie down. Put your feet up. Just do nothing for a while. Tiredness will signal you to stop and take note of what is happening inside you physically. It may also warn you of what may potentially happen if you don't slow down and allow your body needed time to repair.

Just as a thermostat regulates the temperature of the rooms in your home, physical rest regulates our level of harmful stress on our bodies. When our bodies are rested, we respond much better to life's daily stress—"the normal psychological and physical reaction to positive or negative situations in life."[7]

We need *some* stress in our lives. Good stress gets us out of bed in the morning, gets our "physical motors" running and ready to work. But much of the stress women experience today is harmful and can take a toll on their bodies. Experts tell us that harmful stress (and our reaction to it) can cause us headaches, back pain, chest pain, heart palpations and heart disease, high blood pressure, decreased immunity, stomach upset, sleep problems, and a host of other physical ailments.[8]

We respond to and cope with stress differently when our bodies are well and rested and prepared to meet the challenges most days inevitably bring. But when we are tired, overworked, and depleted of energy, even the smallest stressors can bring titanic overreactions that harm us physically. "When we are under severe strain, maybe resulting from an accumulation of small stresses—bills, work pressures, irritating habits of family members—suddenly every minor frustration hits like a blow. We have become hypersensitive, and our minds are telling us we need a respite as surely as neuronal hypersensitivity warns our bodies of a need for relief."[9]

And if we aren't alert and careful, those day-after-day repeated little irritations and frustrations and other stresses build up to major confusion and chaos. Karl Menninger writes: "The repetition of minor irritations and frustrations may be cumulative in their effects to a disturbing degree."[10]

Without regular mental and emotional rest and relief, the minor stresses add up to the point they can affect us in the same ways an earth-shattering event might devastate us.

THE HUMAN BODY AND HARMFUL STRESS

Let's look at how the human body reacts to stress. Imagine you are walking in the park on a beautiful day, enjoying nature, and getting some exercise. As you walk, a large snarling dog jumps into your path, teeth bared and growling. You sense you are in big trouble because it looks like the dog will attack you. Without any thought or effort on your part, your God-endowed physical survival gifts immediately take charge. Your brain shouts: "Danger!" Your heart races and beats wildly against your chest. Your blood pressure soars and floods your brain and large muscles with extra blood for greater alertness and strength. Your blood sugar rises to supply your body with more fuel. You see your very survival may depend on what you do next. Will you fight the dog or will you run away? In either case, you'll need greater mental alertness to make the life-saving decision, extra strength and fuel to fight or run, and all the rest of the chemical changes that have kicked in to help you physically survive. God equipped most all living creatures with these amazing, automatic, physical life-saving responses to danger.

Let's say you decide to fight the dog, and you win. The dog whimpers, turns, and runs away. You may feel drained after the situation passes and you are once again safe from the dog's attack. But your body will soon return to normal. The danger has passed. You continue your walk, thanking God he gave you the amazing survival skills that have just saved your life.

But suppose that, after the danger has gone, your body continues to stay in the "fight or flight" condition? Imagine living each day with your heart continually racing, blood pressure soaring, your blood sugar rising, and your brain shouting: "Danger!" How long do you suppose you could maintain good physical health?

Many women today live life caught in this highly intense survival mode! It's as if each day brings multiple snarling dogs jumping into their path—the responsibilities of *maintaining a home*—cleaning house, cooking meals, laundering clothes, making repairs, unclogging toilets; the tasks of *working a job*—dealing with employers and coworkers, meeting strict quotas and deadlines; the demands of *marriage*—getting along with a spouse, trying to understand and meet his needs, coping with everyday problems with money, sex, children and/or in-laws; the task of *rearing children*—feeding, clothing, educating, protecting, and teaching them spiritually. Some women have even greater responsibilities, including caretaking for a special-needs child, sick spouse, or aging parent; rearing children as a single mom; or personal health concerns and physical limitations. Each day of life brings a certain intensity, and women race through the hours making urgent decisions, facing dilemmas, enduring disagreements, shouldering a load of work that keeps them physically exhausted, and grabbing fast-food meals that fill their stomachs but don't nourish their bodies. Each night brings the frustration of tired bodies, unfinished tasks, and lost sleep. Each new day brings more work, more problem solving, and more snarling dogs to fight. How can a woman possibly stay well under such continual pressure? "Too much doing, going, helping and giving can take a toll on [women]. . . . Most medical books attribute anywhere from 50 to 80 percent of all diseases to stress-related origins. When I get really busy, I'm quick to cut corners on . . . sleep, exercise and healthy eating."[11]

God never intended his daughters to live in this continual survival mode filled with hectic schedules, deadlines, chaos, and unrelenting noise. "Modern people . . . no longer lead their own lives; they are dragged along by events," wrote Dr. Paul Tournier. "It is a race against the clock."[12] God didn't design us to be dragged along by events or to race against the clock. Instead, he created our bodies to enjoy balance, wellness, and wholeness. When women work too hard, carry too many responsibilities, and try to meet too many demands, they live in a continual state of unease. Day after day, year after year of this fast-paced living will cause them dis-ease. They will get sick and suffer serious health problems. It's just a matter of time.

IT DOESN'T HAVE TO BE THIS WAY!

Our Creator offers us another way to live, to care for our physical bodies. He encourages us to physically rest—deeply, frequently, and diligently.

Jesus himself gives us an example of how and when to rest our bodies. By observing his life, we can learn volumes about the value and importance of physical rest. Jesus had a three-year public ministry that started at about age thirty. He came into a hostile world filled with dangerous people, untreatable diseases, poverty, and physical and spiritual hunger. Jesus freely met the needs of suffering people. Everywhere he went, people crowded around him, pushed against him, and made selfish demands on his time and energy. Jesus preached, taught, healed, and ministered to people under a certain deadline: his upcoming and inevitable crucifixion. He worked hard to choose and train disciples that would continue his salvation work after his death. He had much to do, much to accomplish before his life ended. Yet, Scripture never shows Jesus in a hurry. And when Jesus grew physically tired, he stopped his work and he rested.

Fortunately, Scripture records some of Jesus' rest times. He lay down in the stern of a boat, his head on a cushion, and slept soundly until his storm-frightened, frantic disciples interrupted his much -needed sleep (Mark 4:35–41).

As he traveled through Samaria, he stopped and rested beside Jacob's well and conversed with a troubled woman. (John 4:6: "Jacob's well was there, and Jesus, tired as he was from the journey, sat down by the well.")

And on one particularly busy day, when people surrounded him, they wanted their individual needs met, Jesus stopped his work and just left the scene. Mark tells us that Jesus and his disciples were hungry, and so many demanding people swarmed around them that they had no chance to even eat. In the midst of all the chaos and noise and people, Jesus turned to his disciples and said, "Come with me by yourselves to a quiet place and get some rest" (Mark 6:31). He advised his fellow workers to stop meeting people's needs in the middle of a busy workday, to follow him to a quiet place of solitude, and to rest their tired bodies. That particular verse of Scripture gives me permission to physically rest in spite of the work that calls to be done and the people who seem to so desperately need me. Physical rest is that important!

Mark tells us that Jesus and his disciples purposely escaped the clamoring crowds of needy people, intentionally stepped out of the chaotic situation, got in a nearby boat, and left in search of a solitary place. Jesus' body had signaled to him that he and his disciples needed to cease work and rest—to get off their feet, to escape the noise and mayhem. He listened to his body's need for rest and obeyed it (Mark 6:30–34).

You see, Jesus, the incarnate Word, once suited in human flesh and living on planet Earth, became dependent, as we are, on his body to help him work, meet goals, and help people (John 1:14). Jesus knew that in order to preach, teach, heal, and minister to others, he had to take care of his physical body. He knew that God created the human body to live in an orderly rhythm—work and rest, work and rest. The heart that beat within his very chest reminded him that human life must be lived in a balanced way and that rest is essential to good health. So, when he became physically tired, he stopped work and sought quiet, solitude, and rest.

Physical rest is essential for today's Christian woman. If you and I, as busy women, laden down daily with heavy work and multiple responsibilities, follow Jesus' lifestyle of frequent rest times, we, too, will learn to live our lives in created rhythm and healthy balance. Jesus not only gives us *permission* to rest our bodies, he encourages rest with his own example. He himself shows us when, where, and how to rest.

Practical Suggestions

As you think about your own life, family, and personal health, let me share some practical suggestions with you for resting your body.

- Give yourself permission to physically rest. Study God's Word concerning "rest" and follow Jesus' own example by resting your body when it grows tired. Know that God created your body to work and to rest, to live in wholeness and harmony.
- Learn to recognize your body's subtle signals that encourage you to stop work and rest. Take time during the day to enjoy

"mini-rests." Find a quiet, private place in your home, office, garden, or neighborhood park, and sit down for ten or fifteen minutes. Close your eyes, breathe deeply, and purposely relax your muscles. Ask God to repair your tired body. As you gently stretch and move stiff muscles and limbs—from your feet to the top of your head—thank God for each part of your body. Ask him to strengthen you physically and to replenish your energy, so that you can return to your work with renewed vigor.

- No matter how busy you are, schedule a brief nap during daily work times. Take your thirty minute lunchtime, find a dark quiet place to lie down, close your eyes, and go to sleep. A short nap will make you less stressed and more productive in your work. Avoid, however, taking naps too late in the day, as they may interfere with your night's sleep.

- Get the recommended eight hours of sleep each night. If you suffer from insomnia and are unable to sleep, make an appointment with your doctor or sleep specialist, and seek the root of your sleep problem.

- Rest more often during times of great stress or times when you may anticipate stressful situations: moving to a new house, changing jobs, bringing home a newborn, dealing with financial limitations. Rest will help prepare your body for hard work or trying times ahead.

- Take advantage of unscheduled rest times that might otherwise be upsetting and stressful—such as waiting in a line at the bank or grocery store, sitting in your car while stuck in heavy traffic, listening to a boring person talk, and the like. Purposely relax your muscles and allow your body to rest. Silently commune with God.

- Take care of your body. Learn what foods to eat: foods that will restore and maintain health and that prevent disease. Keep your body warm in cold weather, cool and comfortable in extreme heat, securely fastened in seat belts when traveling, and as safe as possible in all situations.

- Figure out how to scale back on events, dinners, committee assignments, and so on, and allow yourself more personal and quiet rest time. Save your body unneeded wear and tear.

- Talk with employers, family members, friends, your pastor, and others when they ask you to take on more work than you can do. Explain to them your already full work schedule and your need for more physical rest. Be selective in the work you agree to do and volunteer to do.

- If possible, adopt a pet! I have three teacup chihuahuas, Valentino, Penelope, and Alexandra, and have personally learned the huge benefits of owning a loving pet. Specialists tell us, "It only takes 15 to 30 minutes with a dog or cat or watching fish swim to feel less anxious and less stressed. Your body actually goes through physical changes in that length of time that make a difference in your mood. The level of *cortisol*, a hormone associated with stress, is lowered. And the production of *serotonin*, an important chemical associated with well-being, is increased."[13]

- Stretch and exercise your body regularly. Take time to enjoy God's natural creation and refresh your body. Enjoy mildly or non-strenuous hobbies that give you opportunities for physical rest, such as swimming, walking, fishing, or biking, for example.

- Help other Christian women to better understand God's mandate to rest physically. Teach your daughters how and why to rest physically.

Personal Quiet Time to Rest, Study, Reflect, and Pray

1. Scriptures: Please read the following verses:
Mark 6:31–34, especially **Mark 6:31**: "Come with me by yourselves to a quiet place and get some rest."

2. Questions: Please give thought to the following:

Why do you think Jesus told his disciples to go with him and get some rest?

What does Jesus' example—maintaining a balance of work and rest—say to you personally about your own work and rest needs?

3. Prayer suggestions: Pray that God will teach you how to better care for the physical body he created for you. Ask him to help you as you seek to understand the value of regular physical rest.

4. Decisions made (as a result of reading this chapter, studying suggested Scriptures, reflecting upon questions, and praying):

⧽⧼ Group Bible Study ⧽⧼

1. Read: **Genesis 2:2–3**: "By the seventh day God had finished the work he had been doing; so on the seventh day *he rested from all his work.* And God blessed the seventh day and made it holy, because on it he rested from all the work of creating that he had done."

2. Respond: Please consider the following questions and respond to them as a group:

In your opinion, why did God stop his work of creation and rest on the seventh day?

What does his example say to Christian women today about the need to balance work and rest?

3. Share: What have you personally learned from this particular Bible study? What decisions have you made as a result of this chapter and study? What have you learned about rest and the value of taking time to rest that could help others in the group? What suggestions might you give others who work too hard and rest too little?

*NOTE: In this chapter, we examine the type of *tiredness* that women experience when they are multitasking, working too hard, and getting too little rest. If you are experiencing exhaustion beyond the expected "tired," please have yourself checked out by a medical doctor. According to New York City internist Dr. Marianne Legato, chronic fatigue can be caused by a number of health problems, including anemia, poor nutrition, water pills or diuretics, thyroid gland function, adrenal gland function, clinical depression, heart failure, and chronic fatigue syndrome. [14]

Chapter 2

A Woman's Need for Mental and Emotional Rest

Come to me, all you who are weary and
burdened, and I will give you rest. (Matt. 11:28)

꧁ *God gives Christian women his permission to
rest their exhausted minds and emotions.* ꧂

Saturday, December 11, 2004, proved a wonderful and precious
day for my family and me. It also proved one of the most pres-
sured and chaotic days we have ever survived! After much hard work
and dedication, my only son Christian graduated from college. I felt
so proud of him, I could hardly contain my excitement and tears of
joy! At noon that day, I sat with hundreds of other celebrating parents
at Samford University and together we watched our children receive
well-deserved college degrees. My husband and I then took our son out
to lunch, praised him for his commitment and work ethic throughout his college years, and recalled together the special moments of
the ceremony.

By the end of the afternoon, I wanted to go home, take off my business suit and dress shoes, slip into worn snuggly pajamas, and call it a day. But I couldn't. You see Christian and his bride-to-be Rebecca had scheduled a big church wedding and reception at Shades Mountain Baptist Church for that evening. We expected six hundred people, ten bridesmaids and ten groomsmen, and a host of flower arrangers and photographers and musicians. And we needed to personally meet and greet each one.

A college graduation and an enormous wedding all in one day! I raced home after lunch, brushed my hair, refreshed my faded makeup, slipped into an evening dress, and squeezed my tired feet into high-heeled, pointed-toed Cinderella shoes. I arrived at the church just in time for the pre-wedding photographs. With great excitement and tears of joy, I watched my son marry his lovely bride in a beautiful and meaningful wedding ceremony.

Sometime after midnight, I arrived home with 316 leftover chicken fingers and the top of the bride's white-iced wedding cake. I collapsed into bed that night exhausted, my mind and emotions stressed to their limit. Then I lay awake and recalled every tender moment of the wedding. I also thought about the hundreds of thank-you notes I needed to write the next day.

I will use the word "awesome" to describe December 11, 2004. Most women today know what "awesome" means! Awesome means both "wonderful" and "terrible"! I personally knew better than to crowd two important, life-changing events into one day. But this decision was out of my control. I had no choice. Earlier that year, I had gasped when my son told me he wanted to marry immediately after his college graduation.

"Christian!" I joked. "You've got to be kidding! Well, I'll just throw my 'mother-of-the-groom evening gown' in the backseat of the car, and I'll change clothes at the local gas station on my way to the wedding."

Christian didn't laugh. He was serious. He had carved the plans for the day in concrete.

"You do not have full control of all the stress events that occur in your life," Dr. Wayne Oates wrote in his book *Managing Your Stress.* "You do have control over some of the stresses that happen to you. You can spread some of them out by putting more time between the stressful events."[1]

From Dr. Oates, I had learned years before to put some space—at least a day or two, if possible, longer—between major events. One's mind and emotions need time to process important functions, to recall and reflect upon special moments, to linger in memorable spaces, and to simply rest. But my son's plans to graduate and marry the same day were out of my control. I spent the week after in serious recovery mode.

THE OLD TESTAMENT KING DAVID

David records much of his mental and emotional agony, fear, and dis-ease in Scripture's Psalms. When daily stress overwhelms him, he pours his heart out to God.

> Be merciful to me, LORD, for I am faint;
> heal me, LORD, for my bones are in agony.
> My soul is in anguish.
> How long, LORD, how long?
> (Ps. 6:2–3)

In sincere honesty David writes:

> I am worn out from groaning.
> All night long I flood my bed with weeping
> and drench my couch with tears.
> My eyes grow weak with sorrow;
> they fail because of all my foes.
> (Ps. 6:6–7)

In Psalm 22, David cries out:

> My God, my God, why have you forsaken me?
> Why are you so far from saving me,
> so far from my cries of anguish?
> My God, I cry out by day, but you do not answer,
> by night, but I find no rest . . .
> I am a worm . . .
> scorned by everyone, despised by the people.
> All who see me mock me;
> they hurl insults, shaking their heads.
> (Ps. 22:1, 2, 6, 7)

Have you ever felt like that? Have daily stresses accumulated and completely grabbed hold of your mind and emotions and made you feel as powerless, as hopeless, and as overwhelmed as the psalmist David? I have certainly been there at times in my life. How many times have I raised my eyes to God and quoted David's words that begged for relief and escape:

> *My thoughts trouble me* and I am distraught. . . .
> *My heart is in anguish* within me. . . .
> Oh, that I had the wings of a dove! I would fly away and
> be *at rest*.
> I would flee far away. . . .
> I would hurry to my place of shelter,
> far from the tempest and storm.
> (Ps. 55:2–8)

Have you ever wished for "the wings of a dove" so that you could "fly away and be at rest"? Accumulated stress can make us yearn to escape, to respite, to rest our weary minds and emotions.

WOMEN AND JOB STRESS

Employment outside the home proves one area of great stress for many women today. *Job stress* is defined as "a chronic disease caused by conditions in the workplace that negatively affect an individual's performance and/or overall well-being of . . . body and mind."[2]

Women now make up 46 percent of the work force in the United States.[3] Researchers predict this percentage will increase in coming years. In fact, since the recession started and money has become scarce, "a full 82 percent of the job losses have befallen men." Women haven't been affected by job loss like men have. Senior economist at the Center for American Progress Heather Boushey reports, "Given how stark and concentrated the job losses are among men, and that women represented a high proportion of the labor force in the beginning of this recession, women are now bearing the burden . . . of being breadwinners."[4]

More and more women are becoming their family's primary wage earner. Already, 75 percent of employed women work full-time jobs. And some 3.7 percent of employed women work more than one job.[5]

Many of these women are mothers. In fact, "over half of the children born in the United States are born to working mothers."[6]

Stress at work proves a growing problem for women today. In one survey, 60 percent of employed women cited job stress as their number one problem at work. Furthermore, levels of stress-related illness are now nearly twice as high for women as for men.[7]

With recent downsizing and a recession going on, some believe that on-the-job stress has reached near-epidemic proportions in the United States. They tell us that the wear and tear on a woman's body, the constant need to multitask, and the speed at which we push ourselves to work faster, goes deeper than just *feeling tired* and *run down*. They want women to know that "a high-pressure job can actually double [a woman's] risk of a heart attack, and a recent study reveals that chronic work stress can be just as bad on [a woman's] mental and physical well-being as smoking and not exercising. Even working in a noisy office can cause stress hormones to rise to unhealthy levels."[8]

Is Your Job Making You Sick?

Individual women may react differently to job stresses. Some women can deal better than others with the demands of the workplace and the irritations and frustrations it can bring. Much depends on the particular stressors and how long the woman has had to deal with them. Much also depends on the pressure and intensity of the stressors. But the accumulation of frustrating job stresses—without sufficient rest—can damage a woman's health. Medical researchers tell us that job stress can bring insomnia, loss of mental concentration, anxiety, absenteeism, depression, substance abuse, family conflict, and physical illnesses such as heart disease, migraine, headaches, stomach problems, and back problems. [9]

Employment can bring stress from various sources. Some women suffer from job insecurity or a fear of learning new technology in order to keep a job. Others experience ongoing conflicts with coworkers or problems with computer and machine failure. Others may face sexual harassment, petty jealousies, workplace health hazards, irregular work shifts, unpredictable hours, and a host of other problems that cause high stress levels. These problems can weigh on a woman's mind and cause her dis-ease and un-rest.

Many of the women who experience job stress are also wives and moms. They may go to work each day already laden with family frustrations and irritations. Some women lack support at home with the work of children and house. A recent article in the *Washington Post* shows that "in the work-family balancing act, women still do most of the juggling," and "the stress of taking care of family still tends to fall on women, even as more and more women stay in the workforce after giving birth."[10]

Some employed women admit they resent working outside the home and also shouldering most of the workload inside the home.

According to recent data from the government's *American Time Use Survey* analyzed by two economists Alan B. Krueger and Andreas Mueller: "On average, employed women devote much more time to child care and housework than employed men do."[11]

This situation often causes marriage and family problems. In fact, "disagreement over household chores is a major cause of marital conflict and is also associated with more thoughts about divorce. In addition, those who bear an unjust burden are more likely to suffer from depression and a decline in their physical health."[12]

SCRIPTURE'S ADVICE TO OVERWHELMED WOMEN

We can anticipate that a woman's job and home stresses will continue to increase. Stress has become part of a woman's life in our present society. Stress can build and accumulate until it causes physical, mental, and emotional damage to a woman who hasn't learned how to successfully deal with it. But women today have a healing outlet for their stress. They don't have to become a victim of stress, depression, mental exhaustion, and dis-ease. The answer to overwhelming, accumulating, and damaging stress comes to us from God in his Word.

Jesus, himself, invites tired women into his healing presence and promises them soul-rest. "Come to me," he calls, "all you who are weary and burdened, and I will give you rest. Take my yoke upon you and learn from me, for I am gentle and humble in heart, and you will find rest for your souls" (Matt. 11:28–29).

Jesus, himself, gives women the permission and the opportunity to rest their tired minds and emotions through his words and his biblical example. Jesus often took respites in his life on earth. When he grew mentally—and emotionally—weary, he journeyed to the solitude and quietness of a mountain or lake or garden. He took necessary time to pray and ponder, think deeply and reflect. He spent precious hours reconnecting with his life source—his Heavenly Father. He stopped his work, escaped far away from people and problems, and "refilled the cup" he had poured out in self-sacrifice and ministry. With a "full cup," he then returned to his work, to people and their problems.

Have you ever experienced an "empty cup"? Have you ever felt so depleted of mental and emotional energy that you simply had nothing more to give—to your family or to your work? I have. I find I must retreat often to my Heavenly Father to receive renewal, refreshment, and the refilling of my bone-dry cup. I depend on those times of quiet and solitude in order to handle my demanding and difficult workload. Hours spent in the Quiet Place give my life a balance of work and rest, work and rest. They help me to function well and to run the race God has called me to run.

I constantly meet women who are weary and burdened but who refuse to stop and rest. As with a physical respite, they claim they *feel guilty* when they take "valuable work time" to renew and restore mind and emotions. To these women, I tell the Biblical story of Elijah, the great Old Testament prophet, and I relay God's personal instructions to him.

MEET ELIJAH

Elijah serves as a powerful example to emotionally tired women today. God gave Elijah specific advice that rested and restored the prophet's mind and emotions and renewed his hope and sense of purpose. I believe God calls twenty-first-century women to also follow these same divinely given instructions.

Elijah suffered from severe mental and emotional stress and fear. A deeply committed and hard-working prophet, Elijah had called down fire from heaven in a dazzling and frightening display of God's power (1 Kings 18:16–46). After the mighty demonstration that sent witnesses to their knees praising God and rid Mt. Carmel of Baal's false prophets, King Ahab told his wicked wife (a Baal worshipper) Jezebel of Elijah's act. Jezebel then sent a messenger to threaten Elijah's life.

The threat had a disabling effect on Elijah. No doubt, after the event on Mt. Carmel, Elijah's mind and emotions shifted to overload levels. Uncharacteristically, the ordinarily courageous prophet became afraid. Scripture tells us he "ran for his life" all the way to Beersheba in Judah (1 Kings 19:3). He begged God to let him die there in the desert. "I have had enough, LORD," Elijah protested (1 Kings 19:4).

Then, fortunately, Elijah took a good first step. The weary prophet sat down under a tree and fell asleep. As we saw in the previous chapter, sleep proves a powerful healer of body, mind, and emotions. In the quiet place, alone, Elijah slept. Then God sent a food-carrying angel to the prophet. "Get up and eat," the angel told him (1 Kings 19:5). After he ate the bread and drank a jar of water, Elijah lay down again and rested. Again, God sent his messenger, the angel, to feed Elijah, and the prophet ate.

Rest and sleep, nourishing food and water proved the healing recipe for Elijah. Renewed in strength, his mind and emotions fully rested and restored, Elijah stood up and continued his God-directed journey.

I agree with author Stacy Wiebe when she writes, "Too much busyness . . . chafes at the soul. Irritability, frustration, anger, bitterness, burnout and even depression can result. In seeking to serve others, [we women] often neglect our own needs and run out of inner resources from which to draw strength. Spiritually, we become starved. . . . Busyness inevitably affects our relationships. We often don't have energy or time to invest with friends and family."[13]

Elijah's example shows us exactly what to do when we are overwhelmed by events, empty, fearful, and stressed out. It's God's biblical prescription, and God created human beings to combat stress in this sensible way.

ESTABLISH YOUR OWN QUIET PLACE

Every busy woman needs a place to rest her mind and emotions. A place of solitude and quiet, a place that belongs to her, a place where she can answer Jesus' call to "Come to me, all you who are weary and burdened," a place where she can accept his promise: "And I will give you rest."

Do you have such a place in your life? I do. Different seasons of my life have brought me to different quiet places. I now have a beautiful, private, safe garden with large pots of flowers growing beside a porch swing, a tree holding bird feeders, and a fountain that calms me with the sounds of gentle flowing water. I rest often in my garden, a teacup Chihuahua or two tucked under each arm, a cup of warm herbal tea in hand, and the great anticipation of a meeting in solitude with my Father.

At other times in my life, my Quiet Place has been a favorite bedroom chair, a kitchen table beside a window, a bathroom that allowed a few private moments, and an infant's nursery where I breast-fed a baby in the middle of a night. As a girl, I sought the solitude of a tall tree with strong limbs on my grandparent's small farm in northern Georgia. I spent hours cradled in a low tree branch and communing with my Father.

Only during one period of my life did I fail to find a quiet place of solitude. I now look back on those long years in inner city Chelsea, Massachusetts, and I understand why that season of life seemed unusually long and difficult. Located on the edge of Boston, Chelsea proved a type of "armpit" of New England—dirty, smelly, violent, and crowded with helpless, hopeless, impoverished people. My husband Timothy and I lived and worked hard in Chelsea's First Baptist church during our graduate student years. We found no relief from filth, violence, and loud noise during our many years there. Whisky bottles thrown by angry youth shattered against buildings at night. Drug-addicted youth and adults lay face down in their own vomit and refuse during the long days. Crying children, hungry and unguarded, filled the city's streets. The loud sirens of fire engines and police cars screamed and raced throughout the neighborhood. No living green plant grew in Chelsea's concrete grounds. Few youth and adults survived the city's gang violence, alcohol and drug abuse, and poverty. The street became home to whole families who searched trash cans for their daily bread.

Stress after terrifying stress built daily in my head and heart with no way to find relief. No spot in Chelsea provided a quiet place of solitude. At times I placed my hands against my ears and cried out to God, "I can't stand this place! I can't survive another minute here!" But God kept us there, burdened with the heavy needs of people who lived around us, deep in the middle of uncontrolled violence and crime, the victims of repeated home invasions and thefts. Fear ran high in Chelsea. I saw and experienced unimaginable violence. I could find no quiet, safe place to escape, no corner of solitude to rest my weary mind and heart.

Church work in that city proved difficult and demanding. I spent most days working with preschoolers in the church's basement. These children, rescued from abusive homes and dangerous streets, captured my heart. I remember the Hispanic boy, David, a four-year-old who came to the church preschool with deep fingernail cuts behind both ears. I remember toddlers who had been bruised and hurt and came to school crying for help. In the early evenings, after parents had picked up their children, I carried many a crying child home with me when a parent "forgot" they had a son or daughter still at the church preschool.

We, like all Chelsea's residents, somehow survived those difficult days. Just when I thought the situation couldn't get any worse, in October 1973, a fire started in Chelsea's old tire factory. The unusually brisk wind blew the flames in all directions, burning down houses and businesses, and destroying fire trucks and emergency vehicles. Chaos—fire, smoke, screaming running people vacating apartment buildings—lasted into the night. The next morning, most of the city had been destroyed. The new homeless stood with mouths agape and tear-stained faces wondering what to do, where to go. Chelsea's First Baptist church became a refuge for homeless families, as well as a clearing house to sort clothing and food donations that poured in from around the world.

After many years and two graduations, we moved out of Chelsea and headed back South to a teaching position in Louisville, Kentucky. I felt grateful to find trees and green grass and blooming flowers once again. I discovered wonderful quiet places in Louisville to rest my mind and heart in solitude. My thoughts often take me back to Chelsea, however, as I think about and pray for the people who couldn't so easily leave the crowded, violent inner city. Somehow they have stayed, lived out a lifetime there, reared up children and grandchildren—generation after generation.

The Planned Respite

You and I, as busy women, need a quiet place where we can escape into solitude and spend time with our loving Father. Often we can afford only a few minutes in our quiet place, but even a short time can bring renewed strength and hope for tired heads and hearts. At different times in our lives, we may be able to plan longer respites—a day, a week—in places away from home.

In her book *The Spirit of Loveliness*, author Emilie Barnes agrees with me. She writes, "I've come to realize that all people need to get away from everything and everybody on a regular basis for thought, prayers, and just rest. For me this includes both daily quiet times and more extended periods of relaxation and replenishment. And it includes both times spent with my husband and periods of true solitude, spent with just me and God."

Why are these times so important to women today? Barnes writes, "These times of stillness offer me the chance to look within and nurture the real me. They keep me from becoming frazzled and depleted by the world around me."[14]

I truly believe that God encourages Christian women to spend time with him, away from the crowds, away from the demanding work, so that he may refill their empty cups. He invites women today to "be still, and know that I am God" (Ps. 46:10). Scripture convinces me that Jesus himself calls to each of us with the promise of rest from life's weariness and burdens.

Practical Suggestions

If you are weighed down with stress and you suffer from mental and emotional tiredness, here are some suggestions that may help you:

- ♪ Strive to slow down physically. Determine your priorities. Delete all things unnecessary from your daily To Do list.
- ♪ Stop hurrying. Learn to live life without rushing from task to task. Marriage and family therapist H. Norman Wright describes our modern fast-paced lives with the term "hurry sickness." He writes that hurry sickness is a "response that begins to make our internal clocks run faster . . . and faster . . . and faster. As with any illness, specific symptoms reflect the presence of the illness. In the case of hurry sickness, the symptoms are heart disease, elevated blood pressure, or a depression of the immune system that makes you more susceptible to infections and cancer. These conditions are brought on when we exist in a state of stress, pressure, or constant rushing. Even tension headaches, and ulcers are tied to hurry sickness"[15]
- ♪ Refrain from constant multitasking. Concentrate more fully on one task at a time. Multitasking or "concept shifting" occurs when we have to change our focus or shift our attention too frequently. "People can't multitask very well, and when people say they can, they're deluding themselves," said neuroscientist Earl Miller. And, he said, "The brain is very good at deluding itself." Miller, a Picower professor of neuroscience at MIT, says that for the most part, we simply can't focus on more than one thing at a time. What we can do, he said, is shift our focus from one thing to the next with astonishing speed. "Switching from task to task, you think you're actually paying attention

to everything around you at the same time. But you're actually not," Miller said. "You're not paying attention to one or two things simultaneously, but switching between them very rapidly."[16]

ॐ Find a place where you can rest your mind and emotions in solitude. Ask family members to support you as you try to spend more quiet time with God.

ॐ Identify, write down, and evaluate the top ten stressors in your life right now. Figure out ways to de-stress your life in these problem areas.

ॐ Take charge of your time and daily schedule. If possible, schedule major events (such as a trip, graduation, wedding, etc.) with ample rest time between them.

ॐ Know that "the repetition of minor irritations and frustrations may be cumulative in their effects to a disturbing degree."[17] Be alert to mounting stress due to everyday irritations. Combat minor frustrations with solitude and rest before they become a huge problem.

ॐ Carefully choose the foods you eat. Learn what foods make you healthy and what foods destroy good health. Change your diet to include healthy choices. Know that "poor eating habits can have a negative effect on your mood and ability to function. Unhealthy eating habits can cause nutrient and brain chemical deficiencies or erratic blood sugar levels. This can result in depression, anxiety, mood swings, and forgetfulness."[18]

ॐ During particularly stressful times, follow the example God gave to Elijah. Take extra time to rest, to eat healthy food, to get enough sleep, and to depend on God to restore your mental and emotional strength.

ॐ If employed outside the home and if laboring only for a weekly paycheck, think through the advantages and disadvantages of your job. Giving up your employment might not be an option for you right now. But if you have a choice, ask yourself this question: Is your job worth the sacrifices you make for it? Make decisions about employment based on your health, your family, the nature of your work, your lifestyle, and other factors. Author Larry Burkett writes, "The sad truth is that most working mothers sacrifice time with their families with little or nothing to show for it. Most of the average working mother's wages are consumed by taxes, transportation, childcare costs, and clothing. Even when a working mother's income is large enough to substantially add to the family's budget, the surplus is often consumed by an expanded lifestyle."[19]

§ If employed, talk with your husband and children about sharing household tasks that might otherwise be placed on your shoulders. One study shows that "marriages benefit from fairness in allocating household chores because neither partner is resentful of a just distribution of household labor. The entire family benefits when children, too, do their fair share of household chores; the parents benefit by being relieved of some burdens and the children benefit by feeling a part of the family team and by developing good habits and reliable character."[20] Help with household work will give you more time to rest and replenish your energy.

Personal Quiet Time to Rest, Study, Reflect, and Pray

1. Scriptures: Please read the following verses:

   Psalm 55:2–8: *"My thoughts trouble me* and I am distraught. . . . *My heart is in anguish* within me. . . .
   'Oh, that I had the wings of a dove!
   I would fly away and be *at rest.*
   I would flee far away. . . .
   I would hurry to my place of shelter,
   far from the tempest and storm.'"

Psalm 46:10: "Be still, and know that I am God."

Psalm 37:7: "Be still before the LORD
and wait patiently for him."

2. Questions: Please give thought to the following:

Why is it important for me to have a specific place of quiet
and solitude so that I can spend time with God?

How can I learn to "be still" in God's presence and come to
better "know" him?

How will quiet time alone benefit my mind and emotions
and help me deal with overwhelming stress?

3. Prayer suggestions: Pray for inner rest and peace. Pray also
for the busy and stressed women you know who could find
renewal and rest if they found a quiet place and spent time
there with God.

4. Decisions made: After reading this chapter, have you made
any personal decisions about resting your mind and emotions? If so, what are they?

❧ Group Bible Study ❧

1. Read: **Matthew 11:28**: "Come to me, all you who are weary and burdened, and I will give you rest."

2. Respond: Please consider the following questions and respond to them as a group:

   Do you have a place of quiet and solitude? If so, please describe it.

   What do Jesus' words in Matthew 11:28 mean to you personally?

   How does spending time with your Heavenly Father restore and renew your mind and emotions?

3. Share: What have you personally learned from this chapter about rest? Do these biblical suggestions change your mind about rest, quiet places, and solitude? If so, in what ways? How can you help other busy women learn and benefit from these Scriptural encouragements?

Chapter 3

THE TRUSTING SOUL REST

Take my yoke upon you and learn from me,
for I am gentle and humble in heart, and
you will find *rest for your souls.* (Matt. 11:29)

✎ *God gives Christian women his
permission to rest their weary souls* ✎

We've seen that, as busy and responsible women, we need physical rest. Jesus often took time away from his demanding ministry to sit down and simply rest his body. He advised his disciples to follow his example.

We've also seen that physical rest proves just one part of our need for rest. Our weary and overburdened minds and emotions need solitude and quiet and time to mend after life's inevitable daily chaos and irritations. Jesus sought out those quiet places where he could be alone, places that allowed his mind and emotions a much-needed rest.

Now let's look at a different kind of rest, one few people ever talk or write about—the harmony and wholeness of heart that I call *soul-rest.* We can find rest for our souls because we can completely trust our loving Heavenly Father. He has proven that he is a trustworthy Father, in that he gives us his precious gift of soul-rest.

A Dark and Stormy Night

For many years as a young girl, I lived with my mother, father, and younger sister Jill in a suburb of Atlanta, Georgia. My mother had designed and built our house. Outside a set of sliding glass doors in my bedroom, she constructed a long enclosed balcony. I often sat on the balcony and enjoyed the natural beauty around me, studied, or read. It was also a fun place for "hide and seek" with my little sister.

One dark night, a violent thunderstorm broke out. I pulled the bed covers over my head and listened to the pounding rain. That's when I heard the sirens. I jumped from my bed and peeked out the window. Three or four police cars blocked our usually quiet street. Police had their weapons drawn and began spreading out through our yard and our neighborhood. I called out for my father, who slept in the next room.

Daddy put on his clothes, walked outside, and talked to one of the officers.

"A prisoner has escaped, and he was spotted in this neighborhood," the policeman told Daddy. "Go back inside and lock your doors. He could be anywhere. We'll find him."

My father came back inside, locked the doors, and carefully searched every room and closet. My mother, sister, and I huddled together in my bedroom. That's when I heard Daddy say, "The balcony! He may be hiding on the balcony!" It was the only place Daddy hadn't checked.

My father was a big man—over six feet tall, broad shouldered, well muscled. He was a gentleman, well mannered, kind, and soft spoken. I don't remember that he ever lost his temper, raised his voice, or became upset. But Daddy was also an ex-Marine. After his years serving in World War II, he knew how to protect himself and his family. He was strong and he was able to take care of us and keep us safe. I pitied the person that threatened him or his family.

Daddy walked to the sliding glass door of my bedroom. Without hesitation, he opened the door and stepped onto the balcony. I held my breath, not knowing what would happen if the escaped prisoner was hiding there. But I also felt a sense of peace. Whatever happened, I knew my father could handle it. He would not allow any harm to come our way. Lightning flashed and thunder clapped as he opened the glass door. Rain pelted him as he searched the dark corners of the balcony. After a few minutes, Daddy stepped back into the bedroom. He was soaking wet, but he had good news. "There's no one hiding on the balcony."

After a few hours, the police cars turned off their flashing red lights, and disappeared as quickly as they had appeared. I don't know whether they ever caught the prisoner or just gave up their search. I fell asleep that night and slept soundly, knowing that my father would watch over me, my mom, and my sister. He was able. He loved us, and he'd protect us from danger.

Soul-Rest

You and I can experience *spiritual heart-rest* or *soul-rest* because we know we have a Heavenly Father who loves us, protects us, and is able to handle anything that comes our way. Our Father oversees and guards every aspect of our lives. He's always watching and loving us. We can sleep peacefully even when chaos and upheaval surround us because we have his assurance we are never alone. He lives with us.

Whereas physical rest involves the physical body, mental rest involves the brain, and emotional rest involves the gut, soul-rest involves the heart. This is precisely what Jesus means when he said: "Do not let your *hearts* be troubled. Trust in God; trust also in me" (John 14:1 NIV 1984). When we know our Heavenly Father is in control of us, our loved ones, our world, and our universe, we can live from day to day with untroubled and peaceful hearts.

The Heart—The Center of Life

In biblical days, people designated the *heart* as the center of a person's life, one's intelligence, and one's thought processes, as well as one's feelings, emotions, and affections. When feeling sad or discouraged, "one claimed an anxious heart weighs a man down" (Prov. 12:25 NIV); a despairing heart brings him pain and grief and meaninglessness (Eccles. 2:20-23 NIV) and a "sorrow hath filled your heart/heavy heart" (John 16:6; Prov. 25:20). People placed the emotions of love (Mark 12:30; 1 Tim. 1:5 HCSB) as well as hate, jealousy, envy, and bitterness within the scope of one's heart (Lev. 19:17 RSV; James 3:14). Morality was measured in terms of "heart." Heart and "conscience" proved interchangeable words for people of that time (1 Sam. 16:7 RSV; Jer. 17:9 NASB; Matt. 15:19). People believed God's truth in their hearts, loved God with all their hearts, and believed that God dwelled in their hearts through the gift of the Holy Spirit (2 Cor. 1:22; Eph. 3:17; Rom. 5:5).

Christians continue to use the "heart" terminology two thousand years later. We give our hearts to God through Christ's sacrifice on the cross; we love God with all our heart; the Holy Spirit lives in our hearts and guides our hearts toward righteousness and godly living. When the disciples encountered the risen Christ on the road to Emmaus, they responded with burning hearts (Luke 24:32).

Paul uses "heart language" when he points out that the believer can possess an untroubled heart. Even though people lived with trouble all around them, Paul writes to the Philippians, "The *peace* of God, which transcends all understanding, *will guard your hearts* and your minds in Christ Jesus" (Phil. 4:7).

Peace of heart is a rest, a freedom from disturbance, from noise, conflict, anxiety, and distress. But heart-peace is more than a safe distance from war, conflict, and chaos. It is a continual harmonious state of mind and heart. Peace gives us a *tranquil* heart, a heart that beats in harmony and confidence. Paul writes to the Corinthians, "For God is not a God of disorder but of peace" (1 Cor. 14:33). That sense of heart-peace comes to us as a gift from God. He offers it. We, as his children, can accept and live the gift or reject it and live with a troubled heart and a restless soul.

Peace isn't just possessing the *feeling* of wholeness and harmony. Peace is a fact. It's like the word "love." God promises us the fact of loving us whether or not at any particular moment we "feel" loved. Feelings have little to do with peace or love. They are God's promises to us regardless of our human feelings at the moment. We can know peace in our hearts because Christ promises us his continual presence through the Holy Spirit.

The writer of Proverbs stated with certainty that "a heart at peace gives life to the body" (Prov. 14:30). Peace played an important role in biblical days. Hebrews met and greeted each other with the word *shalom. Shalom* translates into a deeper word than our word "peace." To the Hebrews, it meant a harmony of life, a wholeness and unity of life.

Paul uses the deeper meaning of heart-peace when he begins his letter to the Ephesians: "Grace and *peace* to you" (Eph. 1:2). And he even cites the reason for this peaceful heart when he writes "from God our Father and the Lord Jesus Christ." The unbeliever could never fathom the peaceful rest God gives to the believer's heart, the soul-rest he gives his children. Paul points out that this peace from God transcends all human understanding. It is a gift from God to those who love him, believe in his Son Jesus, and have chosen to die to self and live for him and in him.

When Paul writes to the Colossians, he tells them to "let the *peace* of Christ rule in your *hearts*, since as members of one body you were called to *peace*" (Col. 3:15). Harmony, wholeness, and balance belong to the hearts of believers in Christ and to the members of his body.

Paul ends his letter to the Thessalonians with these words: "Now may the *Lord of peace* himself give you *peace* at all times and in every way" (2 Thess. 3:16).

Human beings yearn for harmony of heart, but the world doesn't offer this type of deeper peace—the wholeness of a peaceful heart wrapped in the Savior's love. It belongs only to those who belong to Jesus. Christ gives believers a spiritually healthy heart and a spiritually peaceful soul.

Jesus makes his followers a promise: "Peace I leave with you; my peace I give you. I do not give to you as the world gives. Do not let your hearts be troubled and do not be afraid" (John 14:27). He promised those who faithfully served him in his days on earth that he would send them another (the Holy Spirit) that would take up residency in their hearts and provide them with a 24/7 presence of peace.

TRUSTING GOD AS FATHER

I find it easy and natural to trust my Heavenly Father. Why? Because I had a Christ-following human father who loved me, protected me, and was genuinely concerned about me. I trusted my dad until the day he died and went to be with the Lord.

But I also know that not all women had dedicated and dependable human fathers as little girls. These women often project the image of their deadbeat dads onto their understanding of God the Father. If their human father was emotionally distant or abusive or undependable, they may unconsciously attribute these undesirable traits to their Heavenly Father as well.

In my recent book *Learning to Trust Your Heavenly Father (Even If You Can't/Couldn't Trust Your Human Father)*, I write about a woman named Marty. She had been hurt deeply in her childhood and youth by an uncaring, harsh father. She suffered from the memories of his abuse for many years. The pain she endured left her with little or no capacity to trust others. Though her father's abuse was long past, it exerted a powerful influence on her present life.

Perhaps the most devastating effect of a father's abuse on his daughter is how it can horribly distort her view of God. My friend Marty couldn't imagine that her Heavenly Father could be loving and nurturing. That's what we do when we are little girls. We look at our human father to teach us about our Heavenly Father. Whether for good or bad, dads often paint portraits of the Heavenly Father for their little girls. And, without intervention and transformation, inept earthly fathers can often influence a girl's life, faith, family, and future for as long as she lives.

Only through intensive Scripture study, prayer, counseling, and Christian friends did Marty come to understand that God, her Heavenly Father, was nothing like her human father. As she studied the attributes of God, Marty began to see a true picture of God. She dipped her brushes into the paint of Scripture and created a more accurate portrait of her Heavenly Father.

THE BELIEVING HEART'S STATE OF PEACE

I once read a beautiful story that so perfectly portrays a Christian believer's state of peace. A rich man commissioned three artists to paint a picture of peace. The first artist presented the man with a mountain scene with snow-capped peaks against a blue sky. The second artist gave him a beautiful ocean scene with a tranquil, blue sea and white sandy beach. To both artists the man complimented the peaceful paintings.

The third artist painted a violent waterfall, the water crashing hundreds of feet on the rocks below. "How is this peaceful?" the man asked. "The sound of the water is deafening and turbulent."

"Look closer," the third artist said, "look behind the waterfall and you'll see a cleft in the rock and a bird perched in that cleft." The rich man leaned forward and noticed the peaceful bird in his secure nest. Then he understood the artist's intentions.

You see, we live in a world of noise and chaos and rushing activity—somewhat like the constantly crashing waterfall. But in the midst of the turmoil, we possess a peaceful place in Jesus, our cleft in the rock, our shelter in the storm.[1]

THE SAFE CLEFT

Jonathan Edwards describes this heart-peace known only by Christian believers: "The strength of a good soldier of Jesus Christ appears in nothing more than in steadfastly maintaining the holy calm, meekness, sweetness and benevolence of his mind, amidst all the storms, injuries, strange behavior and surprising acts and events of this evil and unreasonable world."[2]

Even in the midst of turmoil, the Christian believer can possess a rest of heart and soul that will bring about calmness, meekness, sweetness, and many other Christ-given attributes.

Christ serves as a symbol of peace in many countries of the world. I have not yet traveled to Argentina or Chile, but, one day when I do, I want to see the bronze statue of Christ that stands twenty-six feet high on the Argentina-Chile border between Mendoza and Santiago in the Andes Mountains, more than twelve thousand feet above sea level. The statue, called *Christ the Redeemer of the Andes*, represents peace between the two once warring nations that battled over boundaries but finally concluded mutual peace proved the only way to preserve their countries. Both nations made and molded the statue from the metal of old Argentine cannons they once used to shoot to destroy each other. In Christ's left hand, they placed a cross. They raised his right hand in a blessing. They dedicated the statue on March 13, 1904. At the base of the statue, at Christ's feet, in 1937 they added these words in Spanish: "Sooner shall these mountains crumble into dust than the

Argentines and Chileans break the peace sworn at the feet of Christ the Redeemer."[3]

The metal statue of Christ is an outward symbol of peace, one that united the two warring countries together in peace. How much more valuable and safe from war and danger is the inner heart-peace that Scripture describes—the soul-rest he gives his children.

God Works for Our Good

The Christian believer receives another heart-rest from God's Word, the promise that whatever happens to her, God will work in some way for her own good. Paul writes, "And we know that in all things God works for the good of those who love him, who have been called according to his purpose" (Rom. 8:28). Anxiety and worry have no place in the believer's heart. God is in control of her, her loved ones, and her world.

God welcomes us to ask him directly for those things we need. "Which of you," he asks, "if his son asks for bread, will give him a stone? Or if he asks for a fish, will give him a snake? If you, then, though you are evil, know how to give good gifts to your children, how much more will your Father in heaven give good gifts to those who ask him" (Matt. 7:9–11). Through God's gift of prayer, you and I can converse with the One who created us!

Spiritual rest or soul-rest is knowing a loving Heavenly Father is in control of every aspect of a woman's life and that she can completely trust him. Soul rest also means that she can know with certainty that God loves her and promises to bring good results from the bad things she might experience on a daily basis.

For the believer in Christ, God has already given a trusting soul-rest. Think about this: Scripture tells us that God controls our lives and, in fact, the very universe. This is a form of rest that nonbelievers do not have. We can rest in the fact that God is in control of our lives and our planet and our entire universe. And Scripture tells us that

God loves each of his children—he has our best interests in mind in all that he allows to happen to us. God invites busy women today to find rest for their souls in him.

Find your secure nest from the turbulent world. Live in the harmonious *shalom* that Christ offers you, the safe cleft God has ordered for you. I love the verse in Isaiah that promises you and me rest in the Lord, the unchanging rock eternal. Perhaps this verse should stay on our lips as we go about a busy and stress-filled day:

> You will keep in perfect peace
> those whose minds are steadfast,
> because they trust in you.
> Trust in the LORD forever,
> for the LORD, the LORD himself, is the Rock eternal.
> (Isa. 26:3–4)

A little girl can turn out her bedroom lights and sleep securely when she knows her loving father is in the house. She knows her father is strong and powerful and in full control of her home. Everything must pass by him before it can reach her, and she can know safety and security because he loves her, guards her, and cares for her well-being. Likewise, a Christian woman can rest in the assurance that her powerful Heavenly Father loves, guards, and cares for her. God is in control of her life, her home, her family, and her world. She need not be anxious or worried about the future or for her loved ones. God's presence and protection is always resting in *the back of her mind*. She also knows that whatever tragedy or heartbreak she experiences, God will, in some way, bring good out of it, no matter how bad the situation. This "knowing" brings soul-rest, the sense of peace and security and certainty to her heart she can rely upon.

Practical Suggestions

Perhaps you are plagued by fear, anxiety, and worry, and have not yet found the heart-peace and soul-rest that Jesus offers. Maybe you want to build a stronger faith and trust in God in order to experience an uninterrupted soul-rest. If so, here are some suggestions that may help you:

- Make a list of Scripture verses that encourage you to rest your heart and mind in God's promises. Some of those verses may be John 14:1 (NIV 1984): "Do not let your hearts be troubled. Trust in God; trust also in me." Philippians 4:7: "The peace of God, which transcends all understanding, will guard your hearts and your minds in Christ Jesus."

- Place your written Scripture verses in a place you most often use—at your office desk, on the table by your bed, in the kitchen, and so on. Read them often. Memorize them. Repeat them frequently to yourself aloud. They will strengthen your heart and encourage you when you face frustrations, problems, and life's inevitable daily crises.

- Examine often the state of your heart and soul. Stop and breathe deeply when you feel afraid or frustrated or confused. Think through what situation confronts you. Measure the amount of stress it brings you. Pray the Scriptures that assure you that God loves you, that God is in control of this very situation, that you can trust God as your caring and concerned Heavenly Father. Then, in prayer, give your heart-troubles to him. Let go of the fear, anxiety, and worries you hold in your heart and mind. Let God alone carry them. Give them up to him with the prayerful request of the peace and security and soul-rest he promises to give you.

꙳ When you face unexpected crises, repeat in your heart Paul's encouraging words to the Romans: "And we know that in all things God works for the good of those who love him, who have been called according to his purpose" (Rom. 8:28). They will bring you strength and encouragement when you most need it. They remind us that, as Christians, we never face crises alone. God the Father faces them with us and brings us through them.

꙳ Concentrate on your human father. Make a list of his qualities and his faults. Compare your list with your mental image of God the Father. How are they alike and/or different? Study God's Word to receive a full and genuine portrait of the Heavenly Father.

꙳ When the gifted Charles H. Spurgeon preached his sermon on "Spiritual Peace," February 19, 1860, he reflected on Jesus' promise in John 14:27. He told his congregation that accepting and believing in Christ's death and resurrection offers us soul-rest and peace with God. He also wrote of the peace we must have with our own conscience. He compared both types of peace in a metaphoric way. *"Peace with God is the fountain, and peace with conscience is the crystal stream which issues from it."* Spurgeon believed this type of soul-rest peace is "founded upon a rock, and though the rains descend, and the winds blow, and the floods beat upon that house, it shall not fall, because its foundation is secure."[4] Contemplate what Spurgeon means when he addresses "peace with conscience."

꙳ Share with others the soul-rest and heart-peace you have found as a child of God, as a believer in Christ. They will see Christ in your face, sense your inner calmness, and draw near to you when they, too, face troubles.

Personal Quiet Time to Rest, Study, Reflect, and Pray

1. Scriptures: Please read the following verses:

   Romans 8:28: "And we know that in all things God works for the good of those who love him, who have been called according to his purpose."

   Philippians 4:7: "The *peace* of God, which transcends all understanding, *will guard* your hearts and your minds in Christ Jesus."

   John 14:27: "Peace I leave with you; my peace I give you. I do not give to you as the world gives. Do not let your hearts be troubled and do not be afraid."

   Matthew 11:29: "Take my yoke upon you and learn from me, for I am gentle and humble in heart, and you will find *rest for your souls*."

2. Questions: Please give thought to the following:

   What situations in my life bring me fear and anxiety? How can I face them with trust in God? What fearful and anxious situations can I avoid? What situations do I need to invest myself and cannot avoid?

   What is the state of my heart right now? Anxious, frustrated, worried, afraid? What exercises can I do that will point me to God's soul-rest and heart-peace? Stop and pray? Read and meditate on God's reassuring Word? Learn to give God my troubles and trust deeply in him?

What does complete "trust in God" mean to me personally? Do I really believe that God, my loving Heavenly Father, is in complete control of every situation I face? Why or why not? How can I strengthen this assurance and trust more deeply in God?

3. Prayer suggestions: Pray that God will give you a better understanding of his love and concern for you. Pray that God will deepen your trust in him as your loving Heavenly Father who brings good to you even from difficult and painful situations.

4. Decisions made: After reading this chapter, have you made any personal decisions? If so, what are they?

❧ Group Bible Study ❧

1. Read: **Philippians 4:7:** "The *peace* of God, which transcends all understanding, *will guard* your hearts and your minds in Christ Jesus."

2. Respond: Please consider the following questions/comments and respond to them as a group:

What is the nature of this soul-rest and heart-peace that "transcends all understanding"?

Describe in your own words the meaning of *shalom*.

How important is it to our heart, mind, soul, and everyday life that God's peace guards our hearts and minds in Christ?

What problems are you currently experiencing (and that you feel free to talk about) that cause you to need special prayer and encouragement? In what ways would you like for your friends in this group to encourage and advise you?

3. Share: What have you personally learned from this chapter? How can you reach out to other Christians with the good news of *shalom*?

Chapter 4

Resting in Prayer

Very early in the morning, while it was still dark, Jesus got up, left the house and went off to a solitary place, where he prayed. (Mark 1:35)

✎ *God gives Christian women his permission to rest in him through prayer.* ✑

Deep nourishing rest comes to Christian women when they can have direct and dependable access to God through prayer.

While living in human flesh, Jesus placed a high priority on praying to his Heavenly Father. Prayer kept Father and Son connected in intimacy and fellowship. I grew up in a Christian tradition and denomination that believes in the importance of prayer. I have heard many beautifully phrased public prayers spoken with all heads bowed and eyes closed in various church worship services. My parents and grandparents taught me to pray with them and others before I ate a meal, before I took a test at school, before I faced a challenge I was uncertain or nervous about, and before I went to sleep at night. Group prayer strengthened me and gave me courage. I have tried to teach these prayer practices to my own children. I have also prayed many prayers aloud in a group setting such as Sunday school classes, women's

Bible studies and retreats, and together with a few close friends. Public prayers are important. We need to pray as a worshipping and fellow-shipping community.

PUBLIC PRAYERS

But public prayers, while essential to a community of faith, aren't the focus of this chapter on women and rest. When Christians pray publicly, they are aware of other people hearing their words. They may shy away from exposing the intimacy of their hearts. Hearts are most often very private places. I find that my personal one-on-one prayers with God give me the intimacy I need, the guidance I seek, and the rest I yearn for. I think Jesus also found the one-on-one prayers with God essential to his faith and life.

In my study of Scripture, I find that Jesus rarely prayed in public. At first, after I made this discovery, I felt surprised. I guess I had never thought about it. But Scripture records just a few public prayers that came from Jesus' lips.

In John 11, when Jesus stood before the rock-barred tomb of his dear friend Lazarus, he prayed a public prayer. Before he ordered the dead man to walk out of his tomb, Jesus raised his voice in prayer, saying, "Father, I thank you that you have heard me. I knew that you always hear me, but I said this for the benefit of the people standing here, that they may believe that you sent me" (John 11:41–42). In this very prayer, Jesus admits his reason for praying aloud—"for the benefit of the people standing here" and so that "they may believe." Then, after everyone had heard his prayer, he called to Lazarus inside the dark tomb: "Lazarus, come out!" (John 11:43). In this Scripture, John gives us the reason for public praying—"for the benefit of the people." And Jesus sets a public prayer example: "so they may believe."

In Luke 9, Jesus prays in public. A crowd of hungry people surround him. He takes five loaves of bread and two fish in his hands and notice-ably turns his face to heaven. Luke tells us "he gave thanks and broke them" (Luke 9:16). Luke doesn't tell us what Jesus prayed or if he used words. But the crowd sat on the ground around him. They no doubt saw him look to heaven in a position of thanksgiving. He had the attention of the crowd when he lifted his head to heaven and gave thanks.

In John 17, when Jesus prayed, at least one person—John—heard him pray. John faithfully recorded Jesus' prayer for us. From a reading of John 16:29–33, we can discern that perhaps some of the other disciples also heard his prayer. Perhaps this public prayer helped better explain Jesus' mission to the disciples, his concern for their safety, and the value of their individual ministries as he prayed for future believers. John tells us that after Jesus' prayer, he and the disciples crossed the Kidron Valley and there met Judas, the betrayer, as well as the arresting soldiers and self-righteous religious officials.

RESTING IN PRIVATE PRAYER

While Scripture shows us some of Jesus' public prayers, we are made most aware of his private talks with God—in the gardens, in the wildernesses, on the mountainsides. From my study of Scripture, I am led to believe that most of Jesus' prayers were intimate, heart-to-heart talks solely between him and his Heavenly Father. Jesus' humanity needed the quiet assurance of God, the rest the Father offered him, and the strength and guidance to continue his exhausting ministry. I believe most of Jesus' intimate prayers with the Father took place away from other people and in the quiet privacy of his own solitude.

Mark tells us that Jesus rose before dawn, sought a quiet place, and spent time there praying alone in a "solitary place" (Mark 1:35–37). I imagine Jesus had little time alone as he ministered to vast crowds and stayed surrounded by his inquisitive disciples. Maybe that's why he slipped out of bed and left the house and found a quiet place to pray in solitude. Mark tells us that Simon and his companions went to look for Jesus. When they finally found him, they exclaimed: "Everyone is looking for you!"

I can understand why Jesus slipped away in search of a quiet place. At times in my own life, it seemed I had no personal quiet time to myself. Someone was always "looking for me." Maybe you feel that way too. I find that most Christian women yearn for quiet time alone to study God's Word and to talk with him one-on-one. Women come to treasure these private moments with God, for they can be rare in the life of an overextended career-worker, wife, mother, grandmother, and so on. Women need intimacy with their Heavenly Father in order to face their responsibilities, cope with all those who need them and their services, and seek guidance in so many areas of the lives they lead.

No doubt, Jesus treasured the times and opportunities when he could slip away (escape) to quiet places, talk with his Father, and enjoy the rest that prayer can provide.

NOT ALL PRIVATE PRAYER IS RESTFUL

Not all private prayers in quiet places are restful, however. Some of our prayer times in solitude are hard work, times when we confess our faults and sins to God, times when we struggle with a problem and his answer to the problem, times when we wrestle with God in prayer. Sometimes the "resting in prayer" doesn't happen during the prayer but after the struggling prayer is finished.

For instance, Matthew tells us that after John baptized Jesus, Jesus slipped away to the wilderness for forty days to be alone with God and pray. The wilderness is a frightening place. In those days, people associated the desert with struggle in prayer with God. A place of danger, one had to keep watch and always be on guard when alone in the desert. Most people believed the desert to be the home of demons and wild beasts. When I visited the Judean Desert, I was told about the numerous poisonous snakes there. I cannot imagine being there alone at night. The desert was not a place I cared to linger. In the Judean Desert, a rugged landscape, deep canyons and rivers, mountains and steep cliffs surrounded Jesus. Satan appeared to him, testing and tempting him. Scripture tells us that Jesus had nothing to eat, and he became very hungry. After a period of wrestling and struggling in prayer, when Jesus rebuked Satan and quoted Scripture to the tempter, he proved his undeniable faithfulness to God and to his mission. He didn't give in to Satan. He stood his ground. When the devil left him, Matthew tells us that angels came and attended him (Matt. 4:11). After the hard work of prayer was over, Jesus found his rest. After forty days, he left the wilderness, and with a prayer-prepared heart, he began the work of his public ministry.

THE WRESTLING PRAYER

Have you ever struggled and wrestled in prayer? I have many times. Did God reward you in your struggles? I find that when I wrestle in prayer, when I agonize in conversation with my Heavenly Father, he rewards me with a new peace of heart. Sometimes we must know the hard work of prayer before we can enjoy the restfulness of prayer and intimacy with God. Jesus had a three-year, dangerous ministry ahead of him. He used the hard work of prayer in the isolated desert to prepare himself to serve God with devotion and faithfulness.

Scripture records another long agonizing prayer Jesus prayed in solitude. In the Garden of Gethsemane, before his arrest and crucifixion, Jesus "fell with his face to the ground and prayed" that the cup of painful death be taken from him (Matt. 26:39). Again Jesus reveals his devotion and faithfulness to God's plan. After he wrestled in prayer, after he struggled in solitude, he accepted God's will and proved faithful to God's plan. Surely he found a certain rest after his decision was made.

Aside from his prayer-struggles, Jesus knew the necessity of finding quiet places to spend time alone with God when he needed to rest his mind and emotions, make important decisions, and talk with his Father about what troubled his heart.

Prayer respites gave Jesus clarity when he needed to make decisions. They gave him strength and courage when he faced difficult and deadly situations. They gave him opportunity to pour out his heart and his tears to the One who loved him and listened to his sorrows, his fears, and his sufferings. But most of all, prayer respites gave Jesus time to be with God the Father. Whether he worked hard in agonizing praying or simply asked God's will to be done, prayer gave Jesus time to know that he existed in God's plan, in God's care, in God's hands.

That's the *rest* prayer brings. You and I can know with assurance that we can call on God and he will be there, loving, caring, and listening to us. The act of praying may not always be restful, but the fact that God is always available for you and me is the rest prayer provides.

Rest also results when you know with certainty that he will guide you in your decision making and encourage you in your sufferings and sorrows and that he is totally in control of every aspect of your life. That's the gift of prayerful rest. You and I can communicate with our Heavenly Father anytime and anywhere. He is our Creator, the One who knows us inside and out, who knows our thoughts, our actions, our concerns, and our fears. He gives us the priceless opportunity to talk with him, and to gain deeper faith, devotion, and greater understanding of life and faith. And more than that, he not only *listens* to us, but he also speaks to our hearts. A permanent and significant rest comes in knowing our Father is only a heart-whisper away whenever we need to talk or cry or plead. Surely, rest comes in knowing a loving Father stays close by—in us, around us, before us, behind us—and waits for us to come to him in intimate prayer.

PRAYERS FROM SCRIPTURE

Prayer is the golden thread that weaves itself in and out and throughout the New Testament. Scripture shows us that prayer is essential to Christ-believers—the vine that nourishes the growing fruit-bearing branch. Saul, who became Paul after his dramatic conversion on the Damascus Road, in his letter to the Galatians tells how he trekked to Arabia for three years before he returned to Damascus and Jerusalem to begin his public ministry (Gal. 1:15–17). Perhaps he spent this time alone in deep prayer and ministry preparation.

Paul lived a life of prayer. He preached prayer! In his letter to the Philippians he told them, "Do not be anxious about anything, but in everything, by *prayer and petition*, with thanksgiving, present your requests to God" (Phil. 4:6 NIV 1984). He told the Colossians to "devote yourselves to prayer" (Col. 4:2). Both James (James 1:5) and Peter (1 Pet. 4:7) encouraged prayer.

Scripture also records the prayers of Old Testament people of God. The barren Hannah prayed when she couldn't conceive a child. She poured out her heart to God in prayer. She prayed agonizing prayers: "In bitterness of soul, Hannah wept much and prayed to the LORD" (1 Sam. 1:10 NIV 1984). Hannah prayed from her heart silently. God answered Hannah's prayer for a son, Samuel (1 Sam. 1:20).

After King David's sins of adultery and murder, he prayed that God might

> create in me a pure heart, O God,
> and renew a steadfast spirit within me.
> (Ps. 51:10)

David admitted to God that his sin had broken both his spirit and his heart (v. 17). He came humbly to God with a contrite heart (v. 17)—a guilty, remorseful and sorrowful, regretful, penitent/repenting heart. Like David, when we sin, prayer offers us a place to sort things out with God, to put things right again, to gather guidance and strength to face the uncertain future. God through prayer gives us another chance, a cleansed and pure heart.

Perhaps the most interesting prayers are from the psalmists. The psalmists argued, complained, demanded, begged, and fought when they prayed (Pss. 5, 6, 7, 17, 22, etc.). They left nothing unsaid. Others prayed humble prayers for greater and deeper belief and dedication like this one:

Search me, O God, and know my heart;
test me and know my anxious thoughts.
(Ps. 139:23)

The psalmists exploded in prayerful praise of God and his creation (Pss. 18, 19, 21, 27, 33, etc.).

THE GIFT OF PRAYER

You and I, as Christian women, have been given the gift of prayer by God himself. We can know with confidence that we can come to God at any time and for any reason. He is dependable. That knowledge provides a rest for our soul, a security that God loves us and is available to listen and respond to us in prayer.

Jesus spent much time away by himself and in prayer with his Heavenly Father. He gives us his example that we, too, can make prayer a priority in our lives. Jesus taught his disciples all about prayer. His teachings are as appropriate for us now as they were for his disciples.

Jesus emphasized private prayer. "And when you pray, do not be like the hypocrites, for they love to pray standing in the synagogues and on the street corners to be seen by others.... But when you pray, go into your room, close the door and pray to your Father" (Matt. 6:5–6).

Do you have a private place to pray? A place where you can close the door and spend solitary time with God? A place where you can pour out your heart to him and not be heard or disturbed by others? Jesus encourages us to find a private place where we can talk to him alone and without distraction.

Jesus also suggested our prayers be simple. "And when you pray, do not keep on babbling like pagans, for they think they will be heard because of their many words" (Matt. 6:7). We aren't giving an eloquent speech when we pray. We are simply talking with our Creator, the One who knows what we need before we even ask.

Jesus recommended private, intimate, and simple prayers. This is the type of prayer he gave us as an example. When his disciples pressed him for a prayer formula, he gave them about fifty simple words (Matt. 6:9–13). That's all. He didn't give them volumes, just a few sentences.

PERSISTENT PRAYING

Jesus also taught his disciples to be persistent in prayer. He told them two most unusual stories about how we are to persist in prayer. One was about an elderly widow who became nagging and persistent when a judge refused to give her justice. I never understood this strange story until I placed it in the context of persistent praying. Then it made sense. God wants us to come to him again and again and again with our request, our plea, and to be persistent to the point of nagging. But unlike the unjust judge, he is the just judge. Amazing! Read the story in Luke 18, think about this story as it relates to our praying, and then see the beauty in Jesus' teachings on prayer.

The second unusual story also suggests great persistence in prayer—prayer that simply does not give up until an answer comes. Jesus told about a friend who needed bread for another friend. The friend went to the neighbor at midnight and demanded food. He didn't give up until he got what he wanted (Luke 11:1–8). Jesus had been teaching his disciples about prayer when he told this story. He ended the story with these words: "So I say to you: Ask and it will be given to you; seek and you will find; knock and the door will be opened to you" (Luke 11:9). Perhaps Jesus knew his disciples might give up praying when God waited a while to give his answer. Through these stories, he seemed to say, "Don't give up—pray until you receive your answer."

THE JOHN 17 PRAYER

The prayer Jesus prayed in John 17 is a special gift to us. We are given the insight of his words and thoughts as he spoke openly to his Heavenly Father. Jesus prayed for himself, he prayed specifically for his disciples, and then he prayed for all believers—future believers—for you and for me. Perhaps the *rest* in prayer comes from being able to be honest and candid in our conversations with God. Of not being afraid we won't say the right thing or use the right words. Of being able to talk to him about anything and everything that frustrates and hurts us—honestly and without embarrassment or fear of disclosure.

In the nineteenth century, George Eliot mentioned this type of incredibly honest communion when she wrote, "Oh the comfort, the inexpressible comfort of feeling safe with a person; having neither to weigh thoughts nor measure words but pour them all out, just as it is, chaff and grain together, knowing that a faithful hand will take them and sift them, keeping what is worth keeping, and then, with the breath of kindness blow the rest away."[1]

How wonderful that we can commune with God in this way. Our Heavenly Father gives us this inexpressible comfort and privilege. He gives us a safe place to talk frankly with him. A place to bring our doubts and our dilemmas. We don't need to measure words or weigh thoughts. We can just pour out our frustrated and breaking hearts to God—chaff and grain together. We can go to him with our anger, our questions, our lack of understanding, and even our fury. He listens. He loves. He understands. With great love, he answers our prayers in the way he deems best. We may not understand his answers, but we can always trust his decisions.

Jesus spoke to God in this way. We have a firsthand account in this recorded prayer in John 17 of how earnestly and simply and intimately Jesus spoke to his Creator. He spoke with God as naturally as he breathed. He gives us this prayer as an example of how we, too, can pray and rest in the arms of the One who created us, sustains us, and loves us.

MEDITATION

Meditation walks hand in hand with prayer. While prayer is speaking with and listening to God, meditation is deep thinking, considering, and pondering God. Meditation is the time we draw close to God, we ponder him. Meditation is the art of focusing your mind on a particular thought and allowing God to enlighten, teach, and instruct you through that thought. Meditation demands solitude and quiet. In Psalm 19, David prays that his prayer ("these words of my mouth") and his deep focused thoughts ("this *meditation* of my heart") be pleasing to the LORD (Ps. 19:14).

The writer of Psalm 1 speaks of the righteous man that knows God and "whose delight is in the law of the LORD." In fact, on this law he "*meditates* . . . day and night" (Ps. 1:2).

My friend and spiritual mentor Dr. J. I. Packer describes meditation as "an activity of holy thought, consciously performed in the presence of God, under the eye of God, by the help of God, as a means of communication with God." He writes that its purpose is to "clear one's mental and spiritual vision of God and let his truth makes its full and proper impact on one's mind and heart." While Eastern meditation seeks to empty the mind, Christian meditation "seeks to focus and fill the mind with the truth of God." Christian meditation brings deeper understanding to the mind, as well as deeper truth and joy to the heart.[2]

The psalmist in Psalm 119 begs God to teach him God's "precepts" (laws, rules) so that he might *meditate* on all God's wonders (Ps. 119:27).

Jesus' mother Mary meditated after his birth as she "treasured up all these things and *pondered them* in her heart" (Luke 2:19).

The Ethiopian eunuch sat on a desert road going down from Jerusalem to Gaza and meditated on the book of Isaiah. He focused his thoughts upon the verses and pondered them, trying to figure out their meaning. He read Isaiah's words about "a sheep to the slaughter" and "a lamb before its shearer," and he yearned to understand them. God directed Philip his way. Philip explained the meaning of Isaiah's words and even baptized the eunuch when he requested it (Acts 8:26–40).

Other words we might use to describe meditation are "considering," "studying," "contemplating," "reflecting," and "ruminating." Meditation brings us close to God, and it brings God close to us. James 4:8 tells us to "come near to God and he will come near to you." The psalmist tells us

> the LORD is near to all who call on him,
> to all who call on him in truth.
> (Ps. 145:18)

Spurgeon writes, "There are times when solitude is better than society, and silence is wiser than speech." He then advises, "we should be better Christians if we were more alone, waiting upon God, and gathering through *meditation* on his Word spiritual strength for labour in his service." He also explains that "hearing, reading, marking, and learning, all require inwardly digesting" and "lies for the most part in *meditating* upon it."[3]

A WOMAN'S HEART

Meditation and devotion come from the heart. The heart is where God does his greatest work in a woman's life—the work of *redemption* (salvation) and *sanctification* (setting apart, becoming more like Christ). Through meditation, God makes our hearts ready to show love and compassion to others and sets us apart from the world for a holy purpose. Meditation, communing in the presence of God, is a gift our Heavenly Father gives every believer. Through quiet meditation, we ponder the assurance of Jesus' words in Matthew 28:20, his promise that "surely I am with you always, to the very end of the age." The hidden meditation of a believer's heart produces a rich and exciting inner life, a certain peace and assurance and *rest* the world might yearn for but without Christ cannot understand or manufacture.

God has given Christian women the privilege to approach him at any time, with any concern, through spirit to Spirit conversation—prayer.

Prayer is God's gift to his daughters, the unique opportunity for them to speak with their Creator and to listen to his response. That open invitation to pray and that gift of prayer bring women deep and comforting rest.

Practical Suggestions

Have you discovered the rest that prayer can bring? If not, or if you want to go deeper into the rest God grants through prayer, here are some suggestions:

- Find a quiet place where you can pray and meditate without noise, distraction, and interruption. Visit it daily and enjoy the rest and solitude it brings. Treasure the time you can spend there with God in intimacy and fellowship.
- Ponder the Spurgeon's words: "There are times when solitude is better than society, and silence is wiser than speech." Do you agree? If so, why? Do you enjoy solitude or dread your time alone? Do you consider being alone as loneliness or treasured time?
- In your prayer time, read the following Scriptures, and then sit quietly and ponder them. After a time of meditation, record your thoughts in a private journal.
  - "'Love the Lord your God with all your heart and with all your soul and with all your mind.' This is the first and greatest commandment" (Matt. 22:37–38).
  - "He has made everything beautiful in its time. He has also set eternity in the hearts of men; yet they cannot fathom what God has done from beginning to end" (Eccles. 3:11 NIV 1984).
  - "Is anyone among you in trouble? Let them pray. . . . The prayer of a righteous person is powerful and effective" (James 5:13, 16).

🔊 Reflect on Paul's words to the Thessalonians: "Rejoice always; pray continually" (1 Thes. 5:16–17). Strive to call on God often and throughout the busy workday. Pray silent prayers from your heart continually, in all places, and in all situations. Stay in communion with your Heavenly Father all the time, always aware that he is close to you and knows your every thought.

🔊 Read Jesus' prayer in Matthew 6:9–13. Ponder its simplicity and directness.

🔊 When you pray, mentally visualize Christ sitting beside you. Talk directly to him. Tell him what's on your heart. Speak to him like a friend who listens, loves you, and cares about what you experience in life.

🔊 Scripture tells us, "Do not be anxious about anything, but in every situation, *by prayer and petition*, with thanksgiving, present your requests to God" (Phil. 4:6). Record your current anxieties, the things you are worried about, the problems that are causing you stress and pressure. Then pray about each recorded anxiety and problem and worry. Trust your Heavenly Father to listen, love, and bring some resolve and peaceful rest to you.

🔊 At times during your busy day, find a place where you can sit down, take off your shoes, close your eyes, and just bask in God's presence. You need not say anything. Just be there, enjoy his presence, and open your heart to listen when he speaks to it. Breathe deeply and enjoy the quietness of the moment with God.

🔊 Take time to learn more about prayer through Scripture, books, articles, and other sources. Read books written by Christian authors who have personally struggled with problems, crises, and difficult people and situations and have made remarkable discoveries about prayer through their suffering. (*Learning to Pray When Your Heart Is Breaking* is one example. I wrote the book when a medical mistake at our hospital claimed the life of my father. It describes how to pray in life's tough times, when God seems silent.) Talk with friends who have come through crises and have been strengthened through prayer and meditation. Those who have suffered have much to teach other Christians.

Personal Quiet Time to Rest, Study, Reflect, and Pray

1. Scriptures: Please read the following verses and meditate upon them in your quiet time:

   Matthew 6:19–21: "Do not store up for yourselves treasures on earth, where moth and vermin destroy, and where thieves break in and steal. But store up for yourselves treasures in heaven, where moth and vermin do not destroy, and where thieves do not break in and steal. For where your treasure is, there your heart will be also."

   Psalms 6:9: "The LORD has heard my cry for mercy; the LORD accepts my prayer."

   1 Peter 3:12: "For the eyes of the Lord are on the righteous and his ears are attentive to their prayer."

   Romans 10:10: "For it is with your heart that you believe and are justified, and it is with your mouth that you confess and are saved."

2. Questions: Read the Lord's Prayer recorded in John 17 and then ponder these questions:

   a. When Jesus prayed for himself (at the beginning of the prayer: John 17:1–5), what requests did he make of God?

b. When Jesus prayed for his disciples (John 17:6–19), what did he specifically ask God to do for them? Why did Jesus make this request?

c. When Jesus prayed for future believers (John 17:20–26), what did he want future believers to know?

3. Prayer suggestions: Pray that you might spend more time in prayer with God, in deeper thought and meditation on his Word, and that you may become closer to your Heavenly Father. Pray that your conversation with God will become to you as natural as breathing. Pray that you will visit him often—continually—as you move through your busy day.

4. Decisions made: After reading this chapter on prayer and meditation, have you made any personal decisions or discoveries? If so, please record them.

◦◦◦ Group Bible Study ◦◦◦

1. Read: **Romans 2:12–13,15**: "All who sin apart from the law will also perish apart from the law, and all who sin under the law will be judged by the law. For it is not those who hear the law who are righteous in God's sight, but it is those who obey the law who will be declared righteous. . . . They show that the requirements of the law are written on their hearts, their consciences also bearing witness, and their thoughts sometimes accusing them and at other times even defending them."

Matthew 13:18–23: "Listen then to what the parable of the sower means: When anyone hears the message about the kingdom and does not understand it, the evil one comes and snatches away what was sown in their heart. This is the seed sown along the path. The seed falling on rocky ground refers to someone who hears the word and at once receives it with joy. But since they have no root, they last only a short time. When trouble or persecution comes because of the word, they quickly fall away. The seed falling among the thorns refers to someone who hears the word, but the worries of this life and the deceitfulness of wealth choke the word, making it unfruitful. But the seed falling on good soil refers to someone who hears the word and understands it. This is the one who produces a crop, yielding a hundred, sixty or thirty times what was sown."

Luke 8:15: "But the seed on good soil stands for those with noble and good heart, who hear the word, retain it, and by persevering produce a crop."

Romans 10:8–10: "But what does it say? 'The word is near you; it is in your mouth and in your heart,' that is, the message concerning faith that we proclaim: If you declare with your mouth, 'Jesus is Lord,' and believe in your heart that God raised him from the dead, you will be saved. For it is with your heart that you believe and are justified, and it is with your mouth that you profess your faith and are saved."

Mark 11:23–24: "Truly I tell you, if anyone says to this mountain, 'Go, throw yourself into the sea,' and does not doubt in their heart but believes that what they say will happen, it will be done for them. Therefore I tell you, whatever you ask for in prayer, believe that you have received it, and it will be yours.

Hebrews 3:12–14: "See to it, brothers and sisters, that none of you has a sinful, unbelieving heart that turns away from the living God. But encourage one another daily, as long as it is called 'Today,' so that none of you may be hardened by sin's deceitfulness. We have come to share in Christ, if indeed we hold our original conviction firmly to the very end."

2. Respond: Discuss this statement as a group after reading the Scripture verses above: "A believer's heart is the place where God does his great work of redemption and sanctification." What does this statement mean to you?

3. Share: What have you personally learned from this chapter about resting in prayer and meditation?

Chapter 5

THE HEART-REST

"'Love the Lord your God with all your heart
and with all your soul and with all your mind.'
This is the first and greatest commandment.
And the second is like it: *'Love your
neighbor* as yourself.'" (Jesus, Matt. 22:37–39)

⨳ *God gives Christian women his permission to rest in him
as they show love, concern, and forgiveness to others.* ⨳

n the mornings when I wake up, before I begin my workday, I read
Paul's words to the Colossians in chapter 3, starting with verses 12
through 17. I pray that as I go throughout my busy day, I can keep
Paul's words in my mind and in my heart and practice them as I relate
to other people.

Let's take a detailed look at Paul's letter to the Christians in
Colossae. Paul wrote the letter while imprisoned (probably in Rome,
in the early AD 60s). Paul's wisdom to the Colossians is God's gift to
us today as his daughters. If we take it to heart and practice it, we can
find in its wisdom a deeply comforting and enduring rest.

"Therefore, as God's chosen people, holy and dearly loved, clothe
yourselves with compassion, kindness, humility, gentleness and
patience" (v. 12).

Paul makes clear that his readers know, without a doubt, that God loves them, that he has chosen them to be his own. You and I matter to our Heavenly Father, we belong to him and to his family. We can find comfort and rest in the fact that our Creator so dearly loves us and that we are so important to him.

When Paul uses the word "clothe," I think of a big warm coat that covers every part of my body from head to toe. When my husband and I moved to Massachusetts, I had just celebrated my twentieth birthday and one full year of marriage. We spent the next seven years in Boston, Massachusetts. I clearly remember the ice-cold winters there. They began sometime in October and often we still had a new fresh snow on Mother's Day in May. Coming from the mild climate in the South, I wore few coats for warmth. A sweater or suit jacket kept me as warm as I needed to be during winters in the Southern states. But during our first winter in Massachusetts, cold weather took on a whole new meaning. I remember a coat my mother sewed for me and sent me in early November. It wrapped around me from my neck to my ankles. I appreciated that loving gift when every morning at 6 A.M. I caught a bus, then transferred above ground to a subway, and then walked several blocks to my office building in downtown Boston. The icy wind—they called them "nor'easters"—penetrated me to the bone. My feet were often numb with cold when I arrived at work.

I think this is what Paul means when he writes: "clothe yourselves." Perhaps he envisions a cloak wrapped tightly around a body, one that keeps warmth on the inside and the cold northeasters on the outside.

But instead of dressing for the cold wind and icy weather, Paul advices clothing ourselves with certain qualities of character, traits that Christ brings to the life of one that has decided to give life, heart, and soul to God. Compassion, kindness, humility, gentleness, patience, forgiveness, love, and peace describe the inner life of a Christian in the way she responds to and treats other people.

COMPASSION

We, as Christians, can rest in the great compassion God shows us as his daughters. Compassion means to feel with sympathy the pain someone else endures. Matthew 23:37–38 proves one of the most beautiful portraits of compassion in Scripture. I can envision Jesus looking at the city of Jerusalem with tears in his eyes. He watches people as they scurry around, treating each other with indifference, rejecting his message of eternal life, and killing God's messengers. His heart longs to join the hearts of the lost people, people whose eyes are blinded to the sufferings and misfortunes of others, people who live their daily lives rejecting the truth of God's promises. He cries "Jerusalem, Jerusalem, you who kill the prophets and stone those sent to you. . . ."

God the Father had sent his people many prophets, prophets the people rejected and even killed to silence their message. Jesus knew they had rejected him, too, just as they had rejected the prophets. He also knew a cross awaited him, an agonizing death, a burial. No doubt he wondered, "Why don't these people listen to the Gospel—the good news I have brought from my Father . . . *our* Father? Do they not see that God is here with them now, Emmanuel's feet stand beside them on the same soil?" Luke mentions earlier that the Pharisees came to Jesus and told him to leave the place because "Herod wants to kill you" (Luke 13:31). Jesus knew his time on earth was limited and that people were hurting and lost. He desperately wanted to relieve their pain and draw them into God's kingdom. He saw their restless thirst, but they refused to drink the living water he offered them. They refused the rest his compassion could bring them.

Then Jesus used an image that every woman can clearly identify with—that of a mother and her children—a hen with her chicks gathered under her wings to protect and comfort them. It is a word picture painted with the brush of deep compassion. "How I have longed to gather your children together, as a hen gathers her chicks under her wings, but you were not willing." Just imagine the great security, protection, and rest a chick feels wrapped up in her mother's wings!

Has your sense of compassion for hurting others ever made your heart hurt—I mean physically hurt? Whenever I travel to the city of Rome, I must prepare myself emotionally to see the homeless, disabled, and hurting people who live on the city's dirty streets. They line the sidewalks and alleys, their heads lowered in pain and shame, their dirty hands raised upward in hopes of receiving a few coins. Often they are missing limbs. Many of them raise fingerless hands begging to engage the compassion of those who most often walk silently by them. I fill my pockets with coins, and I give them out until they run out. But it never seems enough. How they would welcome a mother hen with strong wings that would envelop them in love, warmth, and safety. I believe Jesus felt this kind of compassion for the people who rejected him. He held the answer to their search, yet they stopped their ears and walked the other way.

Recently I saw a woman's compassion in action. My good friend, Becky Carlisle, willingly gave one of her healthy kidneys to a man she didn't know. In doing so, she saved his life. She underwent major surgery and spent time in recovery. Becky's genuine Christ-like compassion relieved the suffering of another person in need. In my eyes, Becky is the very definition of compassion.

The opposite of compassion is indifference, a lack of caring when another hurts. Indifference can be characterized by the cruelty of one human to another. Compassion is a godly trait. Surely, in the act of confronting others with our compassion, we can find a satisfying rest. Rest comes when God calls us to show compassion, and we obey him.

KINDNESS

When we think of kind persons, we often use the words "kindhearted" or "warmhearted" or "bighearted" to describe them. A kind person is friendly, caring, and considerate. Kindness is a "fruit of the Spirit"

(Gal. 5:22). Christians should be kind to each other (Eph. 4:32), even if their kindness is met with hostility and hatefulness (1 Thess. 5:15).

My maternal grandmother was kindness incarnate. I spent many wonderful summers with my grandmother ("Mama") and grandfather ("Papa") on their little farm in northern Georgia. Mama was always kind and gracious to others. She made sure that everyone in her community had warm coats and blankets in the winter. She found out who was hungry and who ran short of food, and she prepared large jars of soup made from the vegetables grown in their garden.

I had just turned nine when Mama showed memorable kindness to a little girl who knocked on her front door. When Mama opened the door, she smiled at the ragged child with the dirty face and bare feet who stood timidly before her.

"Good morning," she said. "What can I do for you today?"

Without a word the child held up several soiled dishtowels.

"Are you selling these?" Mama asked her.

The girl nodded her head, her sad eyes focused on the floor of the porch. Mama invited her inside.

"How did you know that those dishtowels are the very thing I need today?" she asked. "Stay here and let me go get some money."

I watched Mama go to the back bedroom and open the small purse where she kept the week's allotted grocery money. I knew she couldn't afford to part with a penny of it and still feed all of us that week. When my grandmother returned, she gave the child a pocket full of coins and said: "This money is for the dishtowels." Then she gave the girl a hand full of money. "And this money is just for YOU!"

That little act of everyday kindness happened fifty-one years ago. For some reason, it made a lasting impression on me. And to this day, whenever I think of my beloved grandmother, I remember her compassion and kindness to that little barefoot girl. I'll bet the little girl never forgot it either.

God instilled within his children's hearts the need to show kindness to others. A kindhearted Christian is selfless and generous, not selfish and greedy. A heart filled with kindness is a heart that has found peaceful rest.

HUMILITY

Jesus himself told his followers,

> Blessed are the meek [the humble],
> for they will inherit the earth.
> (Matt. 5:5)

We find a rest in humility. We no longer need to "prove" ourselves, climb the "ladder to success," or put on a mask and pretend to be who we definitely are not. Rest comes in not having or wanting to impress anyone by our beauty or accomplishments or anything else.

Saul, a very proud man, who became Paul, met the risen Christ on his way to Damascus. Paul was a distinguished Roman citizen, a Pharisee from the tribe of Benjamin. He had been educated by the most brilliant teachers, especially the rabban Gamaliel the Elder. Religious leaders respected him, invited him to their dinner parties, and introduced him as their friend. Paul's education and repute suggests he came from a wealthy and prominent family. He was a leader filled with pride, proud of his success, status, and accomplishments. His life's vocation? Persecuting Christians. He stood by cheering on those who stoned to death Jesus' follower Stephen in Acts 7:54–60.

Christ dramatically changed *Saul*, the prideful, success-driven, violent Roman, to *Paul*, the man filled with love, compassion, and humility. He changed Paul's heart and the direction of his life. Paul no longer bragged about himself and his accomplishments. He boasted only of Christ's accomplishment for humankind. Saul's heart, once filled full with pride and vanity, became Paul's heart filled with selflessness and submissiveness. Christ's importance replaced the sense of

Paul's own self-importance. Paul placed his feet firmly on the ground and looked honestly at himself in the mirror of Christ's resurrection. He saw his true self—apart from his influential family, his accumulated wealth, his success, his status in the Roman community. He saw a mere man, dependent upon God for his very life, dependent upon the work of Christ for his eternal life. And his eye-opening reflection changed his heart, his vocation, his life, and his eternal destination. He became humble. Paul's humility took him to dangerous places, and he faced violent death many times at the hands of others. Yet that didn't stop him. Christ, not Paul's ego, was now his Lord.

Years ago, a pastor introduced himself to me and said, "I am the most humble man you will ever meet." I felt confused. I wondered: Does true humility boast about being humble? A heart filled with Christ's humility is a heart at rest, not a heart that must continually prove its self-importance by boasting of its humility. The old adage is so true: when we become aware of our humility, we've lost it. William Temple believed that "humility does not mean thinking less of yourself than of other people, nor does it mean having a low opinion of your own gifts. It means freedom from thinking about yourself at all."[1]

Pastor Rick Warren reminds us, "Humility is not thinking less of yourself, it's thinking of yourself less."[2] I like that definition!

When God fills a woman's heart with humility, she knows who she is and to whom she belongs. She understands her intrinsic self-worth as a daughter of God. She shows gratitude for the gifts God has given her to do his Kingdom work. A newfound humility replaces her all-important, ladder-climbing ego. Her identity is hidden in Christ, and her heart discovers a peaceful rest.

Gentleness and Patience

When women treat others with gentleness and patience, they show a calm, kind understanding. They remain uncomplaining and composed. People can trust their actions and know that every meeting will be based on respect and a natural even-temperedness. Gentleness and patience are two marks of the believer in Christ. As we look at his life through the Scriptures, we see ample offerings of his gentleness and his great patience.

THE BEAUTY OF FORGIVENESS

In Colossians 3:13, Paul seems to refer to a heart filled with gentleness and patience when he writes, "Bear with each other and forgive whatever grievances you may have against one another" (NIV 1984). He then reminds his readers that we are deeply flawed by sin and we have all been forgiven by Christ. "Forgive as the Lord forgave you." Paul knew that unforgiveness always leads to a bitter spirit, an ugly resentment, and a desire to punish or seek revenge on the offender. No rest or peace can live in a heart infested by the growing weeds of unforgiveness.

Forgiveness is the gift we give to someone who wrongs us or hurts us. The offender does not in any way deserve this gift of forgiveness. When we forgive others, we do so in our own hearts. We forgive for our own sake, not for the sake of the one who hurts us. When Paul writes, "forgive whatever grievances you may have," that covers just about everything.

When I read the Holocaust diaries written by a teenager Nonna Lisowskaya I saw the difference forgiveness played in this young woman's life. Nonna and her large Russian Orthodox family lived in the Ukraine during World War II when German soldiers invaded Russia. The German soldiers brutally murdered her father, her extended family, and her friends, and destroyed her home and possessions. Nonna and her mother Anna ended up on a people-packed cattle car headed for a German concentration camp. During her years of torture and imprisonment, Nonna kept diaries—writing in pencil on small pieces of paper she sewed together with thread. Inside a small pillow tied around her waist, under her dress, she hid her diaries and family photos. Nonna described in her diaries the cruelty of the German soldiers, how they murdered crowds of Jewish people, how a soldier coldly killed a baby, and other acts of brutality. Nonna's mother was sent to another concentration camp in Germany and murdered. Of all her family members, Nonna was the only one that survived. After the war, Nonna left Germany and traveled to the United States. There, in 1950, she met her future husband Henry Bannister, a young naval officer. They married in 1951 and later moved to Memphis, Tennessee. For almost half a century, Nonna kept her Holocaust experience a secret. She didn't tell Henry or her three children. A devout Christian, Nonna chose to forgive her enemies, the soldiers who murdered her family and tortured and abused her and her mother. She took Paul's words to heart when he wrote: "forgive whatever grievances you may have." She lived a life of love and gentleness, patience and compassion. She locked her diaries and family photos in a trunk in her attic and no one knew anything about her suffering in Germany under Hitler and the Ukraine and Russia under Stalin.

Nonna decided to tell Henry about the diaries, her family, and her Holocaust experiences a few years before she died in 2004. She gave Henry permission to have her diaries published after she passed away. I had the honor of working with Henry and the Bannister family and my good friend Carolyn Tomlin, in order to put them into a readable form. Tyndale House Publishers published the book two years ago, titling it *The Secret Holocaust Diaries: The Untold Story of Nonna Bannister*. Nonna's diaries tell her story of horror but also her decision to forgive her offenders. The book became an immediate best seller. I often wonder how Nonna's life would have been had she chosen not to forgive. I would imagine that Nonna's life, if filled with the hatred, bitterness, and resentment of unforgiveness, might resemble young Tamar's life as recorded in 2 Samuel 13.

The Restlessness of Unforgiveness

Tamar was King David's beautiful virgin daughter. Her half brother Amnon tricked her into coming into his bedroom, and then he violently raped her. She pleaded with him to let her go. But Amnon paid no attention to her cries. After he raped her, he told her to get out of his house. He ordered a personal servant to "get this woman out of my sight and bolt the door after her" (2 Sam. 13:17). In those days, rape ruined a virgin's chance of getting married and having children. Amnon had disgraced Tamar. Tamar told her brother Absalom what had happened, and Absalom was furious. He secretly planned his revenge on Amnon and took the shattered Tamar into his own home and cared for her. Two years later, Absalom ordered Amnon to be killed.

Scripture doesn't say that Tamar ever decided to forgive her rapist. It does tell us, however, that "Tamar lived in her brother Absalom's house, a desolate woman" (2 Sam. 13:20). I believe her lifelong desolation came from a restless, unforgiving, bitter heart. She chose to live in misery and emptiness because she decided not to forgive.

Nonna Bannister's life, on the other hand, shows a woman who chose forgiveness over desolation and bitterness. And she lived a happy life of love and joy.

What happens to us when we decide, like Tamar, not to forgive another? Author Philip Yancey writes, "Not to forgive imprisons me in the past and locks out all potential for change. I thus yield control to another, my enemy, and doom myself to suffering the consequences of the wrong."[3]

Why must we, as Christian women, choose to forgive those that hurt us? Because God, in Christ, has forgiven us (Eph. 4:32) and because Christ asks us to forgive others (Luke 6:36).

Alistair Begg writes in *The Hand of God*: "If we are harboring unforgiveness toward someone, we'll find that our usefulness in the kingdom of God is sadly diminished."[4] Why? A heart that harbors the bitterness of unforgiveness becomes an empty, desolate, restless heart. I agree with author John MacArthur when he writes, "Un-forgiveness is a toxin. It poisons the heart and mind with bitterness, distorting one's whole perspective on life. Anger, resentment, and sorrow begin to overshadow and overwhelm the un-forgiving person—a kind of soul-pollution that enflames evil appetites and evil emotions."[5]

THE LOVE THAT NEVER FAILS

After Paul urges Christians to forgive each other, he focuses on love. Love "binds them all together in perfect unity," he writes (Col. 3:14). Compassion, kindness, humility, gentleness, patience, and forgiveness are all wrapped together in limitless love. It's no wonder that he then writes about peace and thanksgiving. "Let the *peace* of Christ rule in your hearts, since as members of one body you were called to peace. And be *thankful*... with gratitude in your hearts to God" (Col. 3:15–16 NIV 1984).

Paul also wrote to the Corinthians about love—"the most excellent way," he called it (1 Cor. 12:31 NIV 1984). He talks about love being patient and kind, humble not proud, forgiving and keeping "no record of wrongs." Love, he writes, "always protects, always trusts, always hopes, always perseveres. Love never fails" (1 Cor. 13:4–8).

Paul ends chapter 13 of 1 Corinthians with these words: "And now these three remain: faith, hope and love. But the greatest of these is love" (1 Cor. 13:13).

A truly rested heart is filled with love, compassion, kindness, humility, gentleness, patience, forgiveness, peace, gratitude, and thanksgiving. These are the virtues the Apostle Paul encourages us to clothe ourselves with, to wrap around our hearts like a warm coat (Col. 3:12–17). A heart filled with God's gifts, such as these, has no room in it to harbor hatred, jealously, envy, unforgiveness, impatience, or bitterness. A busy woman has no time or energy to expend harboring a heart full of bitterness and grudges.

Practical Suggestions

Here are some ways you can follow Paul's words to the Colossians:

- Reread Paul's wise words to the Colossians, found in Col. 3:12–17. For the next five days, choose one of the verses each day to ponder and think deeply about. Decide how you can become more compassionate, kind, humble, gentle, patient, forgiving, and loving to the others around you.
- Think about those people who have somehow hurt you in their words or actions. Think about how you feel towards them. Decide to forgive them in your heart.
- Charles Stanley writes: "Forgiveness is 'the act of setting someone free from an obligation to you that is a result of a wrong done against you.' . . . [It] involves three elements: injury, a debt resulting from the injury, and a cancellation of the debt. All three elements are essential if forgiveness is to take place."[6] Spend some time pondering the meaning of Stanley's statement about forgiveness. Do you agree with him about the "three elements" forgiveness involves? Why or why not?
- As you go about your day, think of how you can show God's love in the forms of compassion, kindness, patience, and other ways.
- Pray and seek wisdom from God about those things you want to improve. For instance, instead of practicing patience, do you often allow your temper to flare up? Could you be kinder to the people around you?
- Consider this statement and record your thoughts: "The choice to forgive, love, and show compassion and concern for others is *intentional*, and it frees a Christian woman's soul to rest and live fully, unencumbered with unforgiveness, bitterness, hatred, envy, and all those other harmful *soul-states* that can cause deep unrest in a woman's life. She can *intentionally choose*

to free herself from these human burdens that can quickly and permanently *cripple and imprison* her soul, as well as *hinder* her ministry to others."

৯ Consider the state of your heart if you choose not to forgive a person who hurts you. Contemplate the words: *revenge, reprisal,* and *retaliation.* Do a word study and reflect on what happens to a woman's heart when she harbors the desire to seek revenge, reprisal, and retaliation.

> ৯ *Revenge* and *reprisal* seek to injure the person who has injured us. When we seek revenge or reprisal, we become avengers who inflict injury.

> ৯ *Retaliation* seeks to return evil for evil—blow for blow, insult for insult, harm for harm.

Personal Quiet Time to Rest, Study, Reflect, and Pray

1. Scriptures: Please read, study, and contemplate:

Matthew 18:21–22: "Then Peter came to Jesus and asked, 'Lord, how many times *shall I forgive my brother* when he sins against me? Up to seven times?' Jesus answered, 'I tell you, not seven times, but seventy-seven times'" (NIV 1984).

Matthew 22:37–39: "Jesus replied: '*Love the Lord* your God with all your heart and with all your soul and with all your mind.' This is the first and greatest commandment. And the second is like it: '*Love your neighbor* as yourself.'"

Matthew 15:32 (Jesus' own example of compassion): "I have *compassion* for these people; they have already been with me three days and have nothing to eat."

1 Peter 3:8–9: "Finally, all of you, live in harmony with one another; be sympathetic, love as brothers, be compassionate and humble. Do not pay evil with evil or insult with insult, but with blessing" (NIV 1984).

2. Questions: Please reflect upon and respond to the following:

Why do you think Paul gives us these models (love, patience, kindness, etc.) to live out in our daily lives?

What virtue do you find the most difficult to practice and why?

What is your own personal definition of *forgiveness*? Explain. Contemplate.

3. Prayer suggestions: Pray that God will help you to become more like him in the way you relate to those people around you. Pray that people throughout your daily life can see Christ's love as it lives in your heart and reaches out in love and compassion for others. Pray for all those people who desperately need these attributes in their lives.

4. Decisions made (as a result of reading this chapter, studying suggested Scriptures, reflecting upon questions, and praying):

⤜ Group Bible Study ⤛

1. Read: **Colossians 3:12–17:** "Therefore, as God's chosen people, holy and dearly loved, clothe yourselves with compassion, kindness, humility, gentleness and patience. Bear with each other and forgive one another if any of you has a grievance against someone. Forgive as the Lord forgave you. And over all these virtues put on love, which binds them all together in perfect unity. Let the peace of Christ rule in

your hearts, since as members of one body you were called to peace. And be thankful. Let the message of Christ dwell among you richly as you teach and admonish one another with all wisdom through psalms, hymns, and songs from the Spirit, singing to God with gratitude in your hearts. And whatever you do, whether in word or deed, do it all in the name of the Lord Jesus, giving thanks to God the Father through him.

2. Respond: Questions to consider and respond to as a group:

How does *love* bind all these attributes together (v. 14)?

Define *peace*. Describe the difference between inner peace and world peace.

What might happen to your family, church, and community if every Christian practiced Paul's advice in Colossians 3:13: "Forgive as the Lord forgave you"?

3. Share: Participants can share with the group what each has learned from this particular Bible study and the decisions that each has made.

THE REST FORGIVENESS GIVES

If we confess our sins he is faithful and
just and will forgive us our sins and purify
us from all unrighteousness. (1 John 1:9)

෯෧ *God gives Christian women his permission to
rest in him through his grace and forgiveness.* ෯෧

n the previous chapter, we saw how forgiving others can bring rest to
our spirit and life. Holding a grudge toward someone who has hurt us
takes energy. Living with a bitterness-filled heart can bring us distress
and distraction. Forgiving others brings rest from resentment and our
natural human desire for revenge. A pure heart is a rested heart.

In this chapter, we'll examine the other two types of forgiveness
that we, as Christian women, need in order to find restful peace.

As human beings, we are born into this world with inherited sin
from Adam, as well as with a sin-prone nature. When we look into
our new baby's (or grandbaby's) face, we may find it hard to believe
that humans come endowed with original sin. But Scripture makes
this clear. Paul wrote to the Roman Christians, "Therefore, just as sin
entered the world through one man, and death through sin, and in
this way death came to all men" (Rom. 5:12).

But God is a forgiving God. "For God so loved the world that he gave his one and only Son, that whoever believes in him shall not perish but have eternal life" (John 3:16). When we come to God the Father and ask for forgiveness for this original-Adam-debt we owe and we believe in his Son Jesus as our redeeming Lord, God forgives us and we become a daughter in his family. Our decision to ask God's forgiveness and to believe in Jesus' death and resurrection as our redemption leads us on the path to a restful heart. We can know, without a doubt, that we are part of God's family of redeemed believers. Let me again quote Paul in his letter to the Romans: "But God demonstrates his own love for us in this: While we were still sinners, Christ died for us. Since we have now been justified by his blood, how much more shall we be saved from God's wrath through him!" (Rom. 5:8–9).

We call this miracle of God "salvation" and "redemption." We have been "bought," that is redeemed, by Christ's sacrifice, his death on the cross. Paul tells us that when this redemption takes place, we then die to sin and our old life, and we become alive in our new life with Christ. "The death he died, he died to sin once for all; but the life he lives, he lives to God. In the same way, count yourselves dead to sin but alive to God in Christ Jesus" (Rom. 6:10–11). We can rest in the assurance of our salvation.

Scripture also tells us that nothing can separate us from God's love, that we are his, we belong to his family, and our future, our eternal life, is secure in him. Paul writes, "Who shall separate us from the love of Christ? Shall trouble or hardship or persecution or famine or nakedness or danger or sword? . . . For I am convinced that neither death nor life, neither angels nor demons, neither the present nor the future, nor any powers, neither height nor depth, nor anything else in all creation, will be able to separate us from the love of God that is in Christ Jesus our Lord" (Rom. 8:35, 38–39). Knowing that we will forever be loved by God brings us rest. Knowing that nothing can separate us from God's love brings us peace.

THE BEAUTY OF FORGIVENESS

A woman can know God's forgiveness. She can rest in the fact that he, her Heavenly Father, loves her, guides her, speaks to her heart, and secures her place with him for eternity. Without the knowledge of eternal security with God through Christ, I could never find rest. I would constantly worry about my eternal destination. God gives us this "knowing," this security of life with him when death snuffs out our human life. As a forgiven, redeemed daughter of God through Christ, I can leave my house in the mornings and know that if anything should happen to me, my future is secure. That brings me an ultimate rest like nothing else can. God gives us this gift, this permission to rest in him throughout eternity. (We will talk more about this "ultimate rest" in Chapter 14.)

When I know for certain that I have been forgiven by God, that I am secure in his family as a Christ-believer, I can more freely forgive another person who may purposely and intentionally hurt me or hurt someone I love. Paul tells us that, as believers in Christ, we are to forgive one another: "Forgive as the Lord forgave you," he writes in Colossians 3:13.

The message to forgive one another runs throughout the New Testament. Mark writes, "And when you stand praying, if you hold anything against anyone, forgive him, so that your Father in heaven may forgive you your sins" (Mark 11:25 NIV 1984).

Paul wrote to the Ephesians about forgiving each other, too. "Be kind and compassionate to one another," he wrote, "forgiving each other, just as in Christ God forgave you" (Eph. 4:32).

When Peter asked Jesus, "Lord, how many times shall I forgive my brother when he sins against me? Up to seven times?" Jesus answered Peter, "I tell you, not seven times, but seventy-seven times" (Matthew 18:21–22). In other words, don't ever stop forgiving your brother and sister in Christ!

The Third Part of Forgiveness

We've seen how a woman can know, through Scripture, that God has forgiven her for her original human sin, as well as for her sinful failures. She can rest in the fact that God is her forgiving Father, that he himself has released her from her owed debt.

We've also learned that God expects us to forgive one another just as Jesus forgave those who crucified him (Luke 23:32–38) and Stephen forgave his murderers as they stoned him (Acts 7:54–59).

Now let's look at the third part of forgiveness. As women, we can accept God's forgiveness, and we can forgive a person who purposely hurts us. But how difficult we often find it to forgive ourselves when we do wrong. We can ask for forgiveness from God, but how often we fail to accept it. Scripture tells us that God forgives our day-to-day wrongdoings. We apologize to God, ask him to forgive us, and he forgives us.

> I, even I, am he who blots out
> your transgressions, for my own sake,
> and remembers your sins no more.
> (Isa. 43:25)

In other words, when God forgives us, it is a complete forgiveness. He refuses to holds those wrongdoings and sins against us. He has completely forgiven us. What wonderful rest God gives to us when we know, without a doubt, that he "remembers [our] sins no more"!

But how many women refuse to forgive themselves for their wrongdoings even after God has forgiven them?! We, as women, can sometimes be our own worst enemy! We can carry our blame with us, repeat our offenses again and again in our mind, and thus forfeit that beautiful heart-rest of self-forgiveness. We imprison ourselves with blame and berate our own spirit again and again with self-condemnation.

Scripture gives us the ugly details of David's adultery with Bathsheba and how he planned the murder of Bathsheba's husband.

God shows us through his Word how David suffered in his heart and mind and spirit because he sinned so violently against God.

"For I know my transgressions," David prays to God, "and my sin is always before me" (Ps. 51:3).

David asks God's forgiveness. "Cleanse me with hyssop, and I will be clean," he prays. David admits to God that his wrongdoings have left him in spiritual pain, that his very bones seem crushed, that his heart is heavy and he no longer enjoys a restful and glad heart. He comes to God with a "broken spirit; and a broken and contrite heart" (Ps. 51:7, 17). He begs God to restore his joy and gladness, to create purity in his hurting heart, to allow him to praise him again.

"Restore to me the joy of your salvation," he prays (Ps. 51:12). How fortunate we Christians are that God gave us David's recorded prayer asking God's forgiveness.

God did create within David a pure heart. He forgave the sinful David. He made David "clean." I believe David also was able to forgive himself after he received God's cleansing and forgiveness. Surely he never "held a grudge" against himself after God erased his sin and remembered it no more. David's slate was wiped clean!

We all make wrong choices. We are human. David writes in Psalm 103:

> As a father has compassion on his children,
> so the LORD has compassion on those who fear him;
> for he knows how we are formed,
> he remembers that we are dust.
> (Ps. 103:13–14)

How sad when we continue to punish ourselves for sins God has forgiven. We think, if we can make ourselves suffer enough, we won't feel guilty anymore, or we can somehow forgive ourselves. Guilt builds within us and we feel a certain worthlessness to God, to our families, friends, and ourselves. The guilt has consequences on everyone around us. It can hurt our relationships with our spouse, our children, our fellow church members, our coworkers—everyone on our path and in our life. Holding on to self-imposed guilt and unforgiveness can damage our faith, our joy, and our work in God's kingdom. Unresolved and unforgiven guilt within our hearts can bring us sadness and discouragement and make our hearts restless and joyless. We can beat ourselves up for years for a wrongdoing, or we can confess it to Christ and allow the forgiveness of Christ to release us from the pain of guilt and shame. We must forgive ourselves and find again that inner peace and rest through our Lord Jesus Christ.

As Christ-believing women, we must learn how to accept God's forgiveness for our wrong choices and learn how to forgive ourselves. Only then can we find rest from a nagging guilty conscience, sorrow, and inner grief. Lack of self-forgiveness hinders a woman's relationship with God as well as her personal ministry. We must decide to no longer hold onto seeds of guilt and remorse, for they can grow deep roots in our heart and life. First John 1:9 tells us, "If we confess our sins, he is faithful and just and will forgive us our sins and purify us from all unrighteousness." Once forgiven by the Father, and then forgiving ourselves, we won't need to rehash and dwell on past sins nor wallow in guilt. You and I can know with certainty we are forgiven. We have learned the lessons our own sin has taught us, and we can put this sin and the resulting guilt behind us and get on with our life.

Let us take God at his Word and find rest from the guilt that hinders and condemns. God himself has taken care of it. You and I are forgiven. Now let us move on. For much work needs to be done in this hurting world!

Practical Suggestions

Here are some suggestions to help you rest in the knowledge that God, through Christ, has forgiven you and brought you into his family.

- Study and meditate upon the Scriptures that show you the path to salvation in Christ:
  - Romans 5:1
  - Ephesians 2:8
  - 1 Peter 2:24
  - Acts 10:43
  - Ephesians 1:7–8
  - John 3:16
- Ask God to forgive you of your inherited original sin. Confess your faults, your sins, and your need of him for your redemption, for your salvation. Study his Word for assurance that through Christ's death you have been forgiven, that he has paid off your debt, and that you belong to God's family.
- Spend time with devoted Christians who can help you walk through Scripture and understand its deep meaning.
- Find a Bible-believing, Bible-teaching church and enjoy the support and strength of other Christians.
- Spend time with God in prayer, and continue to read and meditate on his Word.

Here are some suggestions to help you rest in the knowledge that God, through Christ, continues to forgive you when you commit wrong acts and to help you extend his forgiveness to yourself.

- Read Hebrews 10:22 and spend time meditating on it: "Let us draw near to God with a sincere heart in full assurance of faith, having our hearts sprinkled *to cleanse us from a guilty conscience*" (NIV 1984).
- Focus your mind on 1 John 1:9: "If we confess our sins, he is faithful and just and will forgive us our sins and purify us from all unrighteousness."
- Strive to live close to Christ, and obedience to God's Word. Study these verses:

John 14:15: "If you love me, *you will obey* what I command" (NIV 1986).

John 14:23: "If anyone loves me, he *will obey* my teaching. My Father will love him, and we will come to him and make our home with him" (NIV 1986).

⸎ Remind yourself often, especially when you are tempted to rehash your wrongdoings in your mind and build up greater guilt in your heart:

For I will forgive their wickedness
and will remember their sins no more.
(Heb. 8:12)

God's Word as it applies to the Hebrews and God's covenant with the house of Israel, applies to us today as well.

Personal Quiet Time to Rest, Study, Reflect, and Pray

1. Scriptures: Please read, study, and contemplate:

1 John 1:9: "If we confess our sins, he is faithful and just and will forgive us our sins and purify us from all unrighteousness."

Acts 10:43: "All the prophets testify about him that everyone who believes in him receives forgiveness of sins through his name."

Ephesians 1:7–8: "In him we have redemption through his blood, the forgiveness of sins, in accordance with the riches of God's grace that he lavished on us with all wisdom and understanding" (NIV 1984).

Hebrews 10:22: "Let us draw near to God with a sincere heart in full assurance of faith, having our hearts sprinkled *to cleanse us from a guilty conscience.*"

2. Questions: Please reflect upon and respond to:

Have you made the decision to come to Christ, ask for his forgiveness, follow him and obey him, and serve him as Lord of your life? Describe the rest you received after you made that decision.

Do you believe that God, through Christ, has forgiven you of your sins?

Do you spend time with God? Do you ask him to forgive you for your everyday failings and wrongdoings? Does that daily forgiveness bring you rest?

What kind of assurance and rest does God's Word bring you when you know you belong to his family, that he loves you unconditionally, and that he has promised you eternal life with him?

3. Prayer suggestions: Pray that God will give you a special "rest of heart" as you study his Word and meditate on the Scriptures.

4. Decisions made (as a result of reading this chapter, studying suggested Scriptures, reflecting upon questions, and praying):

❧ Group Bible Study ❧

1. Read:

   John 14:15: "If you love me, *you will obey* what I command" (NIV 1984).

   John 14:23: "If anyone loves me, he *will obey* my teaching. My Father will love him, and we will come to him and make our home with him" (NIV 1984).

2. Respond: Questions to consider and respond to as a group:

   How can we, as Christian women, live a life in obedience to God's Word?

   What have you discovered about God's love? About God's promise of eternal life with him?

3. Share: Reader will share with group what she has learned from this particular Bible study and the decisions she has made.

Chapter 7

THE REST OF CONTENTMENT

I have learned to be content whatever the circumstances. I know what it is to be in need, and I know what it is to have plenty. I have learned the secret of being content in any and every situation. (Paul, Phil. 4:11–12)

✒ *God gives Christian women his permission to rest in deep, satisfying contentment of soul.* ✒

Have you personally discovered the deep, satisfying rest that contentment can bring? Contentment means living in a state of satisfaction—a state that brings joy to a Christian woman's heart. Contentment brings a sense of well-being, serenity, and tranquility. It is a resting peace planted deep within a woman's heart. The opposite of contentment is anxiety—the sensation of *being choked*. Anxiety produces worry, nervousness, and extreme unease. A woman who lives with anxiety will experience a knot in her stomach that never goes away, the feeling of being fearful or apprehensive and always troubled. A woman who lives in anxiety will not know rest.

No Christian woman needs to live with anxiety or worry. Jesus himself in Luke 12:22–23, told his anxious listeners, "Therefore I tell you, *do not worry* about your life, what you will eat; or about your body, what you will wear. For life is more than food, and the body more than clothes."

Our society dwells in a state of uneasiness. Men and women spend anxious lives worrying about lack of money, losing a job, how they look, the clothes they wear, and the food they eat. They never seem to have "enough." They always want more than they have, no matter how much they already have. Like a hamster running at full speed on a tin wheel, they never reach the place where they find contentment. They never discover that place where they can announce: "I am content with what I have."

GOLCANDA DIAMONDS

Years ago, in the late 1800s, speaker Russell H. Corwell told of an ancient Persian, Ali Hafed, who "owned a very large farm in India that had orchards, grain fields, and gardens . . . and was a wealthy contented man." But one day a wise man from the East told Hafed about the value of diamonds and how wealthy he would be if he owned a diamond mine. The man told Ali Hafed that one diamond the size of his thumb could buy for him the whole county, and, if he owned a diamond mine, he could place his children upon thrones with his great wealth. Ali Hafed went to bed that night feeling great discontent. Although he had great wealth, he wanted more. He yearned to own a diamond mine.

He decided to sell his farm. He traveled the world searching for a diamond mine he could buy and own. Finally, after many years of weary travel and search for diamonds, he became poor, broken, defeated. He lost his will to live and he killed himself.

One day the man who had purchased Ali Hafed's old farm led his camel into the garden to drink. As his camel put its nose into the brook, the man saw a flash of light from the sands of the stream. He pulled out a stone that reflected all the hues of the rainbow. The man had discovered the diamond mine of Golcanda, the most magnificent mine in all history. From this mine came the rare Hope Diamond, as well as many other valuable stones. Ali Hafed had owned the Golcanda Diamond Mine all the time, right under his feet. Yet, in his search for the world's diamonds—what he thought he didn't have—he died in a strange land, poor and discouraged.[1]

PAUL'S ADVICE TO TIMOTHY

Paul talked with young Timothy about the rest of contentment. He told Timothy, "Godliness with contentment is great gain. For we brought nothing into the world, and we can take nothing out of it. But if we have food and clothing, we will be content with that. Those who want to get rich fall into temptation and a trap and into many foolish and harmful desires that plunge people into ruin and destruction. For the love of money is a root of all kinds of evil. Some people, eager for money, have wandered from the faith and pierced themselves with many griefs" (1 Tim. 6:6–10). Surely, Paul himself had seen the many Ali Hafreds of his world.

We have seen this striving for wealth ruin many people in our society. In such hot pursuit of riches and power and material possessions, they have ruined and wasted their own lives as well as the lives of many other people.

Paul also tells Timothy, "But you, man of God, flee from all this, and pursue righteousness, godliness, faith, love, endurance and gentleness" (1 Tim. 6:11). Value and worth lie in these virtues lived out in our day-to-day lives, not in those material possessions that rust or break down or end up in someone's yard sale the day after our funeral.

We take a rest when we stop striving for what the world thinks is valuable. Only a futile life devotes itself to the acquisition of the world's wealth. Our society rewards the anxious person who strives to climb to the top of the corporate ladder or makes more money than most people can make or comes across as more beautiful or powerful than another person. They call it "getting ahead." It is the race that has no finish line—enough is never enough, and there is no place to stop. Only death or disablement stops the dizzying cycle.

"You say, 'If I had a little more, I should be very satisfied.' You make a mistake. If you are not content with what you have, you would not be satisfied if it were doubled," writes Charles Spurgeon.[2]

THE GIFT OF CONTENTMENT

Contentment comes in two areas: contentment in what we own and contentment in the situation or circumstance we presently face. Contentment doesn't come naturally to us as humans. It is a type of biblical rest that Christian women *must learn*, just as the Apostle Paul had to learn. Paul knew great wealth as a Roman citizen with an influential family and the best education money could buy. He lacked for nothing. But, when Paul came face to face with Christ, his definition of "wealth" changed. No longer did prestige, familial riches, material things, the best food and clothes, and other items that bring a sense of pseudo-happiness, appeal to Paul. Christ became the Lord of Paul's life. In his ministry, as he traveled, witnessed, ministered, and planted churches, Paul often had little to eat and nothing much to wear and lived a life at risk of constant danger, murder, and imprisonment. Yet, he could write these words to the Christians at Philippi: "*I have learned to be content* whatever the circumstances. I know what it is to be in need, and I know what it is to have plenty. I have learned the secret of being content in any and every situation" (Phil. 4:11–12).

Charles Spurgeon tells us that when Paul wrote about his contentment to the Philippians, he was an "old grey-headed man upon the borders of the grave, a poor prisoner shut up in Nero's dungeon at Rome."[3]

CONTENTMENT IN HARD CIRCUMSTANCES

Paul wrote his letter to the congregation in Philippi (Macedonia) as he suffered in prison. A victim of a cruel Roman society that persecuted

Christians, Paul sat in some deep, dark hole surrounded by decaying human bodies and rats gnawing on rotting flesh.

I recently visited one of the prisons that incarcerated Paul. Mamertine is a twelve-foot hole at the foot of Capitoline Hill in Rome that held criminals between the seventh century BC and the late fourth century AD. The ancient historian Sallust described Mamertine Prison as a place where "neglect, darkness, and stench make it hideous and fearsome to behold."[4] Standing down in that hole, some two thousand years later, sent shivers down my own spine.

Surely no circumstance we might face could be as bleak as Paul's when he penned this letter to his beloved congregation. Trapped deep within the earth—hungry, filthy, and anticipating death—Paul wasn't overwhelmed with worry, fear, and despair. The prison became his pulpit—his place to proclaim the Gospel of Christ! From his cell, he wrote letters to the Philippians to strengthen them when they, too, faced difficult situations. Paul gave them hope.

Paul's letter also convinces us not to allow a painful situation like this one to drain away our Christian joy. Surrounded by darkness, putrid air, and piles of human waste, Paul had little reason to rejoice. Yet his profound Christ-inspired joy rose high above his suffocating circumstances. He could still write of courage and unity, of love and self-giving, of obedience and rejoicing.

Paul had long ago learned the difference between Christian *joy* and earth's pseudo-happiness. Paul's joy came from Christ. Even imprisonment could not dampen his God-given joy. Paul kept his eyes focused clearly on Christ, not on the situation surrounding him.

Paul also uses his suffering and imprisonment as a tool to encourage fellow believers. He urged them to "go out into the world *uncorrupted*, a *breath of fresh air* in this *squalid and polluted society*." He told them to "carry the light-giving Message" to people everywhere . . . with "rejoicing" (Phil. 2:14–17 MSG).

Paul could write letters of encouragement because he had become "an apprentice" to Christ through his years of teaching, preaching, and suffering. Paul learned to imitate Christ's own responses to cruel people and painful problems. Even in prison, Paul reached out in love to fellow believers in Philippi and offered them strength for their own perilous journeys.

Paul, like Christ, unselfishly put others before himself. Paul possessed the God-given ability to see beyond his polluted world and into eternity. He kept an eternal perspective, one that allowed him to celebrate Christ's life-giving resurrection with joy and excitement. Paul suffered greatly at the hands of cruel others, but he knew he would spend eternity with Christ. He endured, and, in his suffering, he encouraged fellow believers to also endure. Paul kept his mind on the Lord Jesus Christ who awaited him in heaven, Paul's future eternal home (Phil. 3:19–20). Paul believed God's promise, and, in his darkest days, he held on tightly to that promise. Surely Paul knew that the stars in the universe always shine brightest on the darkest night (Phil. 2:15).

FINDING REST IN DIFFICULT CIRCUMSTANCES

Biblical contentment comes from within our hearts. To be internally satisfied and at rest within means that what happens to us on the outside in external circumstances doesn't destroy our restful joy inside. Contentment lives within a person, Christ, not in the possession of more and more things or in happy pleasurable circumstances. St. Augustine wrote, "God, you have made us for yourself, and our hearts are restless till they find their rest in you."[5]

In his book *God's Passion for His Glory,* Dr. John Piper writes: "Nothing makes God more supreme and more central in worship than when a people are utterly persuaded that nothing—not money or prestige or leisure or family or job or health or sports or toys or friends—nothing is going to bring satisfaction to their sinful, guilty, aching hearts besides God."[6]

Surely, in this life, we can find nothing that brings contentment except a heart that belongs forever to Christ.

Our good friend of many years Dr. Warren Wiersbe writes, "Real contentment must come from within. You and I can not change or control the world around us, but we can change and control the world within us."[7]

A LETTER FROM A PRISONER

On her *Back to the Bible* radio program, author Elizabeth Elliot once told about a letter she received from a prisoner. The man had committed a crime that put him in prison for the rest of his life. During his time there, he came to Christ, and he found a rare contentment in his life, even while incarcerated. He wrote in his letter to Elliot, "I will live here behind these walls my remaining days on earth. Then I shall go meet the Lord on the other side. I don't have anything of value. All I own I can put in 2 paper bags. But I do have something that's worth more than anything in the world and you know what it is, yes you're right—Jesus Christ my Savior."

He ended his letter with these words: "I'm in prison and I am happy because I have Jesus in my heart . . . and I always has [*sic*] a wonderful time here in my . . . cell. I have never been this happy before in my entire life . . . . If that's what it takes to stay strong in the Lord then I rather stay right here. 'Cuz, ma'am, Jesus went through more for me than anything possible I owe Him, my life I can never repay him enough . . . I crave His Way, His Word, and His Will. Praise God they can lock me away but they can't lock Jesus away from me."[8]

Even in prison, living in an . . . cell, this Christian experiences joy and contentment due to Christ his Lord.

We, as Christian women, must overcome the temptation to measure our worth and value with society's yardstick: social status, ownership, physical beauty, popular accomplishments, and so on. Advertisers spend much money and invest much time and energy to keep us discontented with what we have and the circumstances around us. While women must always strive as Christians to develop a deeper intimacy with God, a more loving and giving spirit, and a greater ministry to others, in order to find rest we must intentionally step out of society's "rat-race" of discontentment and dissatisfaction with *unimportant* things and situations.

English Christian evangelist and Biblical scholar A. W. Pink wrote, "Instead of complaining at his lot, a contented man is thankful that his condition and circumstances are no worse than they are. Instead of greedily desiring something more than the supply of his present need, he rejoices that God still cares for him. Such an one is 'content' with such as he has."[9]

HELEN KELLER'S CONTENTED REST

Helen Keller remains one of my most inspiring heroes. Unable to see, hear, or speak, she lived her life in darkness and silence. But even there she found Christ's gift of contentment. She writes, "Everything has its wonders, even darkness and silence, and I learn, whatever state I may be in, therein to be content."[10]

I have visited Ivy Green, her birthplace and family home in Tuscumbia, Alabama. The simple, white clapboard house was built in 1820 by Helen's grandfather, one year after Alabama became the twenty-second state of the Union. Each small room contains a fireplace. The house somehow survived the ravages of the Civil War. In 1954, Ivy Green was listed on the National Register of Historic Places and has been maintained meticulously in its original state ever since.

Born on June 27, 1880, Helen was a healthy child. But at nineteen months of age, she became stricken with a severe illness that left her blind and deaf. Her parents Captain Arthur H. and Kate Adams Keller took Helen to see Dr. Alexander Graham Bell. Soon after that, in 1887, they hired teacher, Anne Mansfield Sullivan. I've strolled the gardens and examined the well-pump where Anne Sullivan, Helen's teacher, miraculously opened up the world of communication to Helen. Anne used the garden well-pump to splash water on Helen's hand as she spelled "water" in a fingertip alphabet. When Helen caught on, when she fully understood the lessons her teacher taught her, she studied hard and amazed everyone with her hidden brilliance.

By age ten, Helen had mastered Braille and had learned to use a typewriter. At sixteen years of age, she entered preparatory school. She graduated cum laude from Radcliffe College in 1904. During her lifetime, she lectured in twenty-five countries on five continents, bringing courage and inspiration to millions of the world's blind and deaf people.[11]

Helen wrote, "The best and most beautiful things in the world cannot be seen or even touched—they must be felt with the heart." Helen Keller understood about rest and contentment. "What I am looking for is not out there, it is in me," she wrote.[12]

ANOTHER INSPIRATIONAL HERO

I've always been inspired by the story of Horatio Spafford, a wealthy Chicago lawyer who died in 1888, when Helen Keller was only eight years old. Spafford had everything in life that most people strive to attain: a thriving legal practice, a wife, four daughters and a son, and a beautiful home. A devoted Christian, Spafford spent time with Dwight L. Moody, Ira Sankey, and other well-known Christians of his day.

At the peak of Spafford's success, when his life circumstances were the envy of many, the couple's young son died unexpectedly. Shortly after that, the Great Chicago Fire destroyed most of his real estate investments. The family needed a vacation to recover from their losses, so, in 1873, Spafford arranged a boat trip to Europe. He sent his wife and daughters ahead of him while he took care of some last minutes business in Chicago. After several days, he received word that the boat had had a collision at sea, and all four of his daughters had drowned. Only his wife had survived the accident.

In a state of deep mourning, Spafford traveled by boat to England and to his grief-stricken wife Anna. The journey by sea gave him time to think and pray. Before his boat docked, he had composed a beautiful hymn of contentment: *It Is Well with My Soul*. Composer Philip Bliss heard the words and put music to them. Sankey and Bliss published the song in 1876, the year Bliss died.

The song speaks of sorrows and trials but also of the rest and peace of Christ in heart-breaking circumstances.

Knowing the story behind Horatio Spafford's sufferings and loss and yet hearing his echoes of contentment even in tragedy—his imagery of *peace like a river*—has given hope to thousands of Christians for many years.[13]

This type of peace and contentment, even in our loss and sorrow, keeps us from wallowing in self-pity. We don't dwell on our difficulties. Instead we are thankful to God for what we do have.

This type of biblical rest also includes a certain felt satisfaction and spiritual contentment with a woman's situation in life. Christian women are often called upon by God to do hard work in difficult places. Rather than seek to escape certain situations, women can find contentment in resting in the center of God's will and can even learn to embrace the difficult, and often unexplained, callings in her life. The Apostle Paul gives women a unique perspective from his own example on this "rest of contentment." Scripture teaches women today that some ministry callings involve the painful "thorn[s] in the flesh" that Paul, himself, constantly experienced (2 Cor. 12:7).

SEARCHING FOR CONTENTMENT

Sometimes we believe that contentment is right around the corner. We work hard to get ready to be content. I remember as a young bride wanting to wait and have children when everything was perfect—when we had enough money, when we lived in the perfect house, when our front lawn boasted the most perfect yard, and when all the closets were perfectly cleaned out. Fortunately, after eleven years of waiting for "perfection" that never came, we had two children, reared them, educated them, and married them to wonderful spouses. We still don't have the closets perfectly cleaned out!

Dr. David Jeremiah writes, "At some point, we all get caught up in our own misguided attempts to find peace and contentment by working ourselves to death." Then he tells the story of a tycoon who came upon a fisherman lying back and just soaking in the sunset.

> "Why aren't you out fishing?" the tycoon asked.
>
> "Cause, I've caught all the fish I need for today," he said.
>
> "Well, why don't you go out and catch more? Make a profit, buy a bigger boat, hire more men, become wealthy. Then you could just sit and watch sunsets."
>
> "What do you think I'm doing now?" the contented fisherman asked.[14]

When a Christian woman finds contentment with God, she can refrain from complaining, wondering, wishing, and so forth and can rest with a kind of "It is well with my soul" contentment.

Practical Suggestions:

If you have not yet discovered the peace and rest Christ brings you through contentment, here are some suggestions that may help you.

- Make a list of the possessions you own that you could easily live without. Then write down all those essential things you own and thank God for them.
- Go to a quiet place and contemplate Paul's words in Phil. 4:12. Ponder "the secret" Paul has learned.
- Write down all those things that cause you worry, anxiety, and unrest in your life. Give those things to God in prayer. Tear

the list into pieces and throw it away. Whenever you begin to worry about those things, go to your quiet place and give them again to God in prayer.

§ What circumstances in your life do you most want to change? Why? Would changing these circumstances bring you greater peace and rest? Why or why not?

§ Ponder the word "envy." (Envy comes from the Old French word *envier*, and from the Latin word *invidia*. These words mean "regarding maliciously" and "grudge." Envy is a feeling of discontentment or resentful longing aroused by someone else's possessions, qualities, etc. It is a strong desire to have a quality or possession that belongs to someone else.) Dr. James Dobson would have us remember that "the grass is greener on the other side of the fence, but it still has to be mowed."[15] Do you envy a friend or neighbor? How is this envy displacing Christ's rest in your heart? Pray that God will release you from this envy and restore his peace.

Personal Quiet Time to Rest, Study, Reflect, and Pray

1. Scriptures: Please read, study, and contemplate:

   John 14:6: "I am the way and the truth and the life. No one comes to the Father except through me."

   Philippians 4:11–12: "*I have learned to be content* whatever the circumstances. I know what it is to be in need, and I know what it is to have plenty. I have learned the secret of being content in any and every situation."

   Luke 12:22–23: "Therefore I [Jesus] tell you, *do not worry* about your life, what you will eat; or about your body, what you will wear. Life is more than food, and the body more than clothes."

2. Questions: Please reflect upon and respond to the following:

Think about your life. How do you regard your possessions? Could you live without them? Does your contentment rest upon what you own or your situation in life? Why or why not?

What is your personal definition of contentment?

Do you agree with Paul's definition of contentment? (See Phil. 4:11–12)

Does worry and anxiety in your life keep you from knowing Christ's gift of contentment and peace? What must you do, what steps should you take, in order to know Christ's peace?

3. Prayer suggestions: Pray that God will fill your heart with contentment, rest, and peace in him. Pray that Christ will show you what needs to happen in your life if you've not yet found contentment.

4. Decisions made (as a result of reading this chapter, studying suggested Scriptures, reflecting upon questions, and praying):

Group Bible Study

1. Read: **John 14:6:** "I am the way and the truth and the life.
   No one comes to the Father except through me."

2. Respond: Questions to consider and respond to as a group:

   Knowing that Christ is "the way and the truth and the life,"
   how can women today find peace and rest in that assurance?

   What do you see around you that most worries Christian
   women today? What causes Christian women anxiety? If you
   could talk to a worried, anxious woman about Christ's rest
   and peace, what would you tell her?

   Dr. Packer writes: "There's a difference between knowing
   God and knowing about God. When you truly know God,
   you have energy to serve him, boldness to share him, and contentment in him."[16] Discuss the meaning of this statement.
   Do you agree with it? Why or why not?

3. Share: Reader will share with group what she has learned
   from this particular Bible study and the decisions she
   has made.

Chapter 8

THE REST OF COMMITMENT

You did not choose me, but *I chose you* and *appointed you* to go and bear fruit—*fruit that will last.* (John 15:16)

◇ *God gives Christian women his permission
to rest in their commitment to him.* ◇

One week before Mother's Day Sunday, my son Christian, sixteen, asked me an unusual question: "Mom, what is your favorite kind of tree?"

I told Christian, "The Bradford Pear tree. I like the way the branches are shaped like a pear."

To my surprise, when I awoke on Mother's Day morning, I saw a dozen new trees planted all over our front yard. Somehow, without my knowing it, my son had managed to buy the baby trees and pack them into his car. During the night, he had dug a dozen deep holes and placed a tree in each one.

"Surprise, Mom!" he jumped in my face and shouted to me that morning. "Happy Mother's Day! I planted you a bunch of Bradford Pear trees last night while you were asleep!"

I thanked him, hugged him, and marveled at how he had managed to do it.

The trees began to grow over the next few years. I noticed they were shaped somewhat differently from the Bradford Pear trees I had seen. Then one summer, I learned why. By the end of August, the trees weighed heavily with pears! Real pears! Somehow Christian had confused his trees. Instead of Bradford Pear trees, he had bought and planted Bartlett Pear trees!

The trees have grown tall and full over the past thirteen or fourteen years. And each year they produce a crop of big hearty green pears that even a professional farmer could boast about. At "harvest time," we gather the family, put protective plastic clothes baskets over each head, place a bed sheet at the tree's base, and shake the limbs as hard as we can. The pears fall from the branches, bounce off our protected heads, roll down our steep driveway and into the street, and the whole George family runs to catch them. It's a sight to behold.

I've learned much about pear-producing trees since that Mother's Day so many years ago. Probably the most valuable insight has been this: a Bartlett Pear tree's main purpose in its life is to produce pears. Year after year, tiny buds appear and began to grow into small pears. During the hot months of summer, the pears grow bigger and rounder until they are either stolen by a squirrel or harvested by the George family. The pear tree doesn't question its role or God's will for its life. Somehow it just knows God has created and programmed Bartlett Pear trees to produce Bartlett pears.

FINDING OUR PURPOSE IN LIFE

Scripture tells Christian women today that each of us has a specific purpose in life. It assures us that God has gifted each of his daughters to produce a certain kind of fruit. As members of Christ's body, we use these spiritual gifts in his ministry for the purpose of his kingdom work (Eph. 4:1–16).

God's Word also encourages us to work hard at using these gifts for God's work. The Apostle Paul writes, "Whatever you do, work at it with all your heart, as working for the Lord, not for men, since you know that you will receive an inheritance from the Lord as a reward. It is the Lord Christ you are serving" (Col. 3:23–24 NIV 1984).

What happens when we discover our God-given gift for ministry? The moment becomes miraculous and memorable. A bright light goes off in our heart and mind when we discover the *treasure* we uniquely possess. I am reminded of author Annie Dillard's response when she first saw the "lights in the tree" at Tinker Creek. She wrote, "I had been my whole life a bell, and never knew it until at that moment I was lifted and struck."[1]

She had at last found her purpose in life, her great gift, her "magnificent obsession" (as my friend and seminary professor, the late Dr. Oates, called it). Like the Bartlett Pear tree, she no longer wondered about what God had created her to do. In one insightful second, she literally "saw the lights" in her own tree and discovered her purpose. And like a bell, she rang!

When we find our purpose, our uniquely God-created gift and we are fortunate enough to practice it full time, we will no longer "work" another day in our life. What do I mean by that strange statement? When Providence ties together our "magnificent obsession" with our life's vocation, we will love the work we do. We will love it so much, in fact, that it will become something other than what we might ordinarily define as "work." We will get up each morning with an eagerness to practice our gift, to do our "work." We will experience a joy in accomplishing our purpose, in "producing our pears." *Making a living* will become truly "living"! We will realize a greater joy than mere work could ever bring to us. We know we would practice our discovered gift whether it paid us money or not. When we commit ourselves to doing God's will and using to the best of our ability God's chosen gift for us, we find rest.

DISCOVERING THE "LIGHTS" IN YOUR OWN TREE

Even though I popped out of my mother's womb with a sharpened #2 lead pencil in my tiny red fist, I spent years searching for my purpose in life. I wasn't particularly good in school. I suffered from severe shyness, and that alone made my school years uncomfortable and dreaded. Even by the time I entered high school, I always chose to fail the class rather than stand up before my classmates and teacher and give a verbal report. I usually sat in the back of the class and trembled with fear that I might be called upon to answer a question or read from a textbook.

An unidentified feeling stirred strongly inside of me, but I couldn't figure out what it was or what to do with it. I yearned to do "it." I just didn't know what "it" was! I felt restless and somewhat empty. "I know God created me to do something special," I often told myself. "But what in the world is it?!"

I had just turned thirty when I, like Annie Dillard, finally saw the lights in the tree. My husband, Timothy, had just graduated—from the twenty-third grade! He had finally, after a decade of marriage, graduated from Harvard Divinity School with his doctorate. I looked forward to him finding a good job and earning enough money to buy groceries. By that time, Timothy had earned his BA, his MDiv, and finally his PhD. I felt that Timothy had been "killing me by degrees"! Our shared experience living and working in inner city Chelsea, Massachusetts had been somewhat traumatic for me. I remember loudly proclaiming, (after we had managed to survive the experience and actually graduate), something like: "My goodness! What an experience! Why, I could write a book!"

Timothy accepted a teaching position at Southern Baptist Theological Seminary, and I did, indeed, write that book! I picked up that #2 lead pencil I had carried around purposely all my life, and I sharpened it. When I touched its tip to paper, I "saw the lights" in my own tree! It was as if someone had lifted me up, struck me, and, like a bell, I rang. At that moment, I, too, knew I was a "bell" and meant to ring. God guided me as I wrote *How to Be a Seminary Student—And Survive*. Somehow we had survived the seminary experience, and I wanted to help other seminarians survive it too! With a one-sentence summary scribbled on a piece of paper, I timidly approached a Broadman-Holman Publishers book editor who happened to visit Southern Seminary's campus. He raised his eyebrows and smiled (a good sign!), told me the idea had promise, and three months later sent me a signed, sealed, delivered book contract! I somehow wrote the book, and it came out a year after I completed it. (I must admit that the unexpected ease of receiving that first book contract spoiled me into thinking it would always be that easy. It hasn't been!)

Some thirty-five years and as many published books later, however, I have no doubt that God called me to write for him. I have already received the "reward" God promised me in Colossians 3:24—the joy I have experienced through crafting words on paper. Yes, it has been hard work, but not really "work" at all.

THE REST OF COMMITMENT

"Vocation" is an interesting word. It comes from the Latin word *vocatio*, and it means "calling." God calls each of us to our life's purpose. For some unknown reason, he doesn't print our purpose on our newborn forehead: "Baby Girl, Denise, Purpose: Writer." I wish he had! How much easier that would have been! But God allows us ourselves to discover and find that calling from him, our magnificent obsession, our purpose for being alive on Planet Earth.

I believe that every Christian deep down wants to discover her gifts for the work of ministry. Mission to a hurting world is the purpose instilled within every Christian's heart. It doesn't surprise me that pastor Rick Warren's book *The Purpose-Driven Life* has sold twenty-five million copies! Life is fleeting, we are made to serve God, and we each want to produce eternal fruit. Perhaps our daily prayer should be: "Lord, please spare me from investing my life in work that brings only temporary results. I pray that you will lead me to the work you created me to do, work that has eternal value and consequences."

Have you found your God-given gift yet? Your magnificent obsession? That mysterious something that urges you to get up in the mornings and keeps you eagerly engaged throughout the day?

The word "commitment" means a "responsibility, obligation, or duty." For the woman who has discovered her spiritual gift and who has been called to vocation by God, commitment takes on a new meaning. Commitment becomes a "dedication, devotion, a loyalty and faithfulness" to a promise made to God to step into his kingdom work, using his specific gift to you to produce the fruit he created you to produce. In that context, a commitment becomes an assurance that you are engaged in the vocation and work God created and called you to do. That kind of commitment and work offers the Christian woman a sense of relief, of rest. She can rest in the fact that she is fulfilling her specific purpose—the work God created and called her to do. She no longer must struggle to discern her purpose in life. She knows what it is, and she does it "with all her heart" because she is "working for the Lord, not for men." She is in the joyful process of already receiving the promised reward (or inheritance) from God. It comes from resting in God's promise and expectation of vocation and from resting in the joy she has in doing it and producing fruit. Rest comes when Christian women serve God with this type of deep dedicated focus, doing work God enabled and equipped them to do, work that has meaning and purpose and is eternal. God gives these women the gift of "running the race" he has called them to run. And they run it with great focus, duty, delight, and perseverance.

REMAINING ATTACHED TO THE VINE

Scripture assures us that God chose us, called us, and appointed us to his great work (John 15:16). He cautions us to remain in him as we do his work in this world. God's Word gives us the image of a strong vine that provides nourishment, sustenance for life, and the means to produce fruit. We, as the branches, are attached to the vine, receiving from the Father everything we need to produce the fruit he has created us and appointed us to produce. We are joined to the vine through the Father's love. He is the One who accomplishes his purpose through us. Without him, we are alone, empty, and unproductive (John 15:5–9).

Remaining attached to the vine also means that we have divine guidance in persevering in our appointed work. Our priority list narrows significantly, and we can, in confidence, evaluate our responsibilities in light of the requests of others for our time, work, and energy. God has given us a certain focus, and we are deeply devoted to the purpose he calls us to.

I am often asked to do work that I am in no way gifted to do. Knowing God has called me to write, to minister to his people through the written and published word, I can more easily decline those requests that hinder or interfere with my God-given vocation. I often tell people: "I'd love to do this work with or for you, but God has called me to meet this book deadline, and I don't have the time or energy to do both right now." When people make requests of me, I depend on my steady attachment to the vine to help me discern the value of the work I'm asked to do. Is it *eternal* work that will fall within my God-given gifts and minister to another person? Or is it *temporary* work disconnected from my giftedness and accomplishing no eternal purpose? These are the evaluations that each Christian woman must struggle with on a regular basis. Agreeing and accepting work not within our area of giftedness is like one of my Bartlett Pear trees trying to produce a Granny Smith apple.

Women can depend on God to help them carefully evaluate their priorities and spend their time and energy on things that will last—the *eternal* versus the things that won't last—the *temporary*. Paul writes about people whose minds are focused "on earthly things." He then goes on to explain: "But our citizenship is in heaven" (Phil. 3:19–20).

We are earthly creatures, but God calls us to do work that will produce heavenly results.

"Martha, Martha"

Jesus stated the concept clearly when he addressed his kitchen-frantic friend, Martha: "'Martha, Martha,' the Lord answered, 'you are worried and upset about many things, but *only one thing is needed. Mary has chosen what is better,* and it will not be taken away from her'" (Luke 10:41–42 NIV 1984).

I've always identified with Mary, the woman who sat at Jesus' feet and soaked up his theological teachings. I like to think of myself as a Mary, not a Martha. Maybe it's because I am somewhat envious of Martha—the woman who could cook. I cannot cook. Never learned how to cook. The motto around my house is: "Where there's smoke, there's supper!" We've had to drive guests to the nearest hospital emergency room after they had eaten the dinner I cooked. I am happy to tell you that we've never lost a dinner guest. All have lived. Few have returned, however, to our home for another dinner party.

You know the Mary-Martha story. Martha busied herself in the kitchen cooking up some dinner for Jesus and his hungry disciples. While Martha baked fig cakes, Mary sat by Jesus' feet and hung onto every word he said. She soaked up his teachings and thirsted for more. All was well until Martha complained that Mary needed to help her in the kitchen. She should have kept her mouth shut. That's when Jesus explained to Martha that Mary had "chosen what is better"—the eternal that "will not be taken away from her."

Not only does Jesus' example and words to Martha release me from the guilt of not being able to cook, but he teaches me the difference between the eternal and the temporary. Jesus' teachings would live in Mary's head and heart forever. She worked at understanding his words and concentrated on how she might apply his words to her everyday life. Martha's hard work, on the other hand, would be eaten in a few minutes, and then (excuse the gritty nature of this statement) flushed. Important as food is to the human body, it is temporary. Surely an uncooked, unpeeled apple is as nourishing to the body as a peeled, cooked apple. Martha had a whole lifetime to cook. Mary, however, had the presence of Jesus and his message for only a very short while. "Mary has chosen what is better."

After Jesus' comment to Martha, I've often wondered if Martha laid down her skillet and untied her apron strings, or if she stormed back into the kitchen still determined to serve Jesus and his disciples the fatted calf. Scripture doesn't tell us. I personally have always hoped that she immediately fell to Jesus' feet, let the dinner burn, and joined Mary for Jesus' Theology 101.

DEEP, SATISFYING REST

I truly believe that when Christian women clear their minds, their calendars, and their agendas of mediocre and forgettable work and focus intently upon the work God has called them to do, they can *rest* in the knowledge they are centered directly in God's will and purpose for their lives. They stay attached to the vine, and they are given the assurance that they are working for eternal, not temporary, rewards. They know who they are serving, and they find deep, satisfying *rest* in that purpose-driven and focused commitment to God alone.

Practical Suggestions

- ✷ If you have already discovered your "magnificent obsession," the gift God gave you to equip you to serve him in his kingdom work, take time to stop your eternal work and thank him. You are indeed fortunate to be able to rest in the assurance of your God-given purpose.
- ✷ If you are still unsure what God has specifically called you to do (*vocatio*), spend time in prayer, asking him to make his will and purpose for you clear. Search the Scriptures, devote yourself to

his Word, and pray for vocational discernment. Know that he has, indeed, specifically gifted you and personally calls you to accomplish his eternal work.

❧ If you believe God has called you to a certain vocation, seek the training you need that will better equip you to serve him with these specific gifts. (When God made known to me that he had gifted me with the crafting of words, I immediately set out to learn everything I could about writing and getting my work published. Thirty years later, I am still learning the art of communicating through the written word.) Check out library books that will help educate you to use your distinctive gift. Enroll into community-sponsored or university classes in your area. Make yourself totally available to God so that he may equip and empower you to serve him.

❧ Once you find your "magnificent obsession," work at it with all your heart. Remind yourself daily that it is the Lord Christ you are serving and that your work for him has eternal consequences and value.

❧ When requests from others threaten to hinder your God-called work, learn how to gracefully and kindly decline their request. Evaluate everything you do and make sure you are on the path to accomplishing your God-called eternal work.

❧ Spend much time in personal prayer to assure remaining attached to the vine. Ask God to strengthen you and empower you as you seek to serve him. Spend ample time in solitude and quiet, listening for God's guidance as he speaks to your listening heart. The Apostle Paul urges you to "devote ourselves to prayer" (Col. 4:2).

❧ Pray for other Christian women as they strive to discern their own God-called purpose in life. Scripture tells us to "teach and admonish one another with all wisdom" (Col. 3:16). Share the wisdom of God's Word with others who need to hear it, those who need Scriptural counsel and prayer as they seek to serve God in vocation.

ᕋ To encourage you, read the biographies and stories of other women throughout history who have served God and others with eternal work.

ᕋ Daily renew your commitment to God and his purpose for your life. Stay close to him, attached firmly to the vine, and allow him to continue to equip and empower you to run your race and stay on the course he has given you.

Personal Quiet Time to Rest, Study, Reflect, and Pray

1. Scriptures: Please read, study, and contemplate:

   John 15:5, 9: "I am the vine; you are the branches. If a man *remains in me* and I in him, he *will bear much fruit*; apart from me you can do nothing . . . as the Father has loved me, so have I loved you. Now *remain* in my love" (NIV 1984).

   John 15:16: "You did not choose me, but *I chose you* and *appointed you* to go and bear fruit—*fruit that will last*" (NIV 1984).

   Luke 10:41–42: "Martha, Martha . . . you are worried and upset about many things, but *only one thing is needed. Mary has chosen what is better*, and it will not be taken away from her" (NIV 1984).

2. Questions: Please reflect upon and respond to the following:

   What is your God-given gift for ministry? How would you describe your own "magnificent obsession?" What has God specifically called you to do?

What kinds of eternal results does your work provide? How do you focus your work on eternal rather than temporary results?

In what ways could you improve your gifts to better serve God? In what ways have you already improved and enhanced your God-given gifts?

3. Prayer suggestions: Pray that God will guide you, empower you, and equip you to better serve him with your specific gifts. Ask God to provide you with opportunities to use your gifts in ministry to others. Pray for those women you know who are seeking to discover their own specific gifts for ministry. Ask God to guide them so they might discover their own "magnificent obsessions."

4. Decisions made (as a result of reading this chapter, studying suggested Scriptures, reflecting upon questions, and praying):

⟨⟨ Group Bible Study ⟩⟩

1. Read:

Col. 3:23–24: "Whatever you do, *work at it with all your heart*, as *working for the Lord*, not for men, since you know that you will receive an inheritance from the Lord as a reward. *It is the Lord Christ you are serving*" (NIV 1984).

Luke 10:41–42: "Martha, Martha . . . you are worried and upset about many things, but *only one thing is needed. Mary has chosen what is better*, and it will not be taken away from her" (NIV 1984).

2. Respond: Questions to consider and respond to as a group:

What does Paul mean when he writes, "Whatever you do, work at it with all your heart"? (Col. 3:23). In what spirit or attitude are we supposed to engage in ministry using our God-given gifts?

What advice might you give Martha about the value of eternal work, if you could speak privately with her? What do you believe Jesus meant in his words to Martha (Luke 10:41–42)?

How can Christian women stay attached to God (like a branch to the vine) throughout the busyness of an ordinary day?

How can Christian women help other women discern and discover their own God-given gifts for ministry?

3. Share: Reader will share with group what she has learned from this particular Bible study and the decisions she has made.

Chapter 9

RESTING IN CARETAKING

The earth is the LORD'S, and everything in
it, the world, and all who live in it. (Ps. 24:1)

᠅ *God gives Christian women his permission to rest*
from ultimate caretaking responsibilities. ᠅

Within days after I gave birth to each of my children, I felt over-whelmed with the responsibilities that came with mother-hood. I knew the very survival of these babies depended on me. I found myself often staring into space and wondering whether I could handle it all. Even though my husband Timothy was a wonderful helper and I had a lot of good friends, I often felt alone in taking care of my children. After each birth, I coped with a deep sense of weariness and depression. I often wondered how any woman could take on so much work and responsibility and do it well.

Motherhood became no easier as the children grew up. With each age and stage of their lives, I faced more difficult decisions and differ-ent types of workloads. Their teenage years, and new drivers' licenses, brought them sudden mobility. I felt a loss of control, and I worried about their safety and the peers they chose. I spent a lot of time in prayer for each of them as they made decisions about dating, college and graduate school, and marriage. Surely motherhood is an amazing journey!

On top of my mother role, I tried to help Timothy in his teaching career. I also had a writing career with article and book deadlines, late-night edits, and speaking invitations in and out of town. And I took care of our home and finances: cleaning, cooking my family's meals, laundry, bill-writing and paying, income taxes, and so forth. I often collapsed into bed at night and tried to mentally organize and prepare for all the details of the next day's heavy schedule.

Fortunately, my career gave me flexibility. As a writer, I could stay home with a sick child when he had to miss a day of school. I could put my manuscript aside when my children came home and take off needed days in the week for school plays, teacher-parent meetings, doctors' appointments, and the like. I was fortunate. A woman working a full-time, away from home, demanding job might not have the flexibility I had. Most mothers do work outside the home, either full time or part time.

"Currently, 71.3 percent of women with children are in the labor force."[1] These mothers must somehow coordinate demanding work schedules with children's schedules and be available for both.

I also had a husband who dearly loved our children and helped with them on a regular basis. A large number of mothers today don't have a live-in and helpful spouse.[2] Among single mothers who are divorced or separated, 45 percent are currently divorced or separated, 34.2 percent have never been married, 19 percent are married (in most cases, these numbers represent women who have married), and 1.7 percent were widowed. Out of the 85.4 million mothers in the United States today, some 9.9 million are single mothers solely responsible for children younger than 18 years of age.[3]

Single mothers must somehow do it all—work, take care of the home, and take on the huge responsibility of rearing children.

Single women, wives, and mothers can face other challenges in day-to-day life beyond the average home, career, and mothering workload.

Several years ago, I wrote a book giving Christian women an opportunity to "speak" publicly to their church pastors. I titled the Zondervan-published book: *What Women Wish Pastors Knew*. For my research, I sent out surveys asking church women to respond to one simple question: "What do you wish your pastor knew?" I expected some response, but certainly not the avalanche I immediately received! I discovered that Christian women today deal with a legion of problems—within and outside their motherhood responsibilities.

PROBLEMS WOMEN CAN FACE

The women who answered my survey passed the surveys to their friends, who then passed the survey to their friends. Women told me about the ongoing spousal abuse in their homes and how they coped with the physical, mental, verbal, sexual, and emotional abuse from a husband. I was amazed with the sheer number of women who wanted their pastors to know they suffered abuse at home.

Many of the wives also admitted their husbands kept "dirty little secrets" and then described his addictions to porn or alcohol or drugs or sex. They admitted they had no one to talk with about this problem. Some of these husbands turned out to be deacons or elders in the church. They kept these addictions a secret because they knew public exposure could harm their family and their church family.

I received letters from women married to convicted child molesters. One woman told me, "Everyone in our neighborhood knows my husband is a convicted molester who did time in prison. Now he is home. By law, he can't even pick up our own children from school due to this conviction." She and her children lived and coped with this shameful and embarrassing situation.

Women told me they were still dealing with the psychological trauma brought about from sexual abuse during their early childhood. It proved for most a secret they told no one and a burden they didn't know how to deal with by themselves.

Other wives told me they had lost a husband, either through death or divorce or desertion. Whatever the reason, most confessed deeply grieving their loss.

I also heard from grandmothers who, for one reason or another, provided full-time child care and guardianship for their grandchildren. The organization Grandparents Raising Grandchildren estimates that close to eight million children in America are being raised by grandparents today![4]

"It's like starting all over again with a new family," one grandmother admitted. "I just don't know if I can handle it all, especially now at my age."

Most of the women, wives, mothers, and grandmothers who responded to the anonymous survey reported that they dealt with a myriad of everyday troubles and that they felt exhausted and physically, mentally, and emotionally drained. Many devoted Christian women also admitted they had become spiritually depleted.

THE ROLE OF MOTHERS

Did you know that "the number of children under age 18 in the United States has grown from 47.3 million in 1950 to 74.5 million in 2009. By the year 2030, that number is expected to grow to 87.8 million."[5] The role of motherhood is definitely here to stay!

I believe motherhood is a wonderful blessing. The experience of bringing a child into this world is a miraculous mystery of creation. But the job also requires incredible 24/7 hard and demanding work! I wonder how many new mothers expected the heavy workload a new baby brings?

"The actual experience of being a mother can be quite different from a woman's expectations of the role. What it comes down to is that caring for a child is a lot of hard work. Being a mother is time-consuming, as well as both physically and emotionally demanding. Yet many new mothers are not prepared for just how difficult caring for a child can be."[6]

Why is the role of mother so difficult and time consuming? "A common reality of motherhood is that a child's problems are also a parent's problems, and that sometimes brings on a feeling of helplessness."

Society today can make the role of motherhood even more difficult, as women are told they can do everything at once and do it all perfectly! "Since most young American women today plan to work after completing their educations, the majority eventually find themselves facing the challenges of managing the conflicting demands brought on by juggling the dual roles of career and motherhood. Balancing work and family isn't easy."[7]

The American Psychological Association reports that "mothers are the world's best jugglers: family, work, money—they seem to do it all. However, all that responsibility can often leave moms feeling overstretched and stressed out."[8]

Women are also more likely than men "to report physical and emotional symptoms of stress . . . such as having had a headache . . . having felt as though they could cry, . . . or having had an upset stomach or indigestion."[9]

The same survey reported that women are more likely than men to "eat as a way of managing stress." APA psychologist Lynn Bufka says, "People who handle stress in unhealthy ways may alleviate symptoms of stress in the short term, but end up creating significant health problems over time, and, ironically, more stress. . . . Mothers often put their family needs first and neglect their own."[10]

One recent survey of U.S. moms with children under six years of age reported that once the mother got the baby home, being a mom, they say, "has been a rollercoaster of demands—from trying to balance conflicting obligations in order to keep their kids on schedule to dealing with public temper tantrums to enduring dreaded diaper changes in public restrooms."[11]

Motherhood—very rewarding and very difficult.

CARETAKERS

Mothers know hard work, making difficult decisions, juggling all the plates of life and not allowing any of them to drop and shatter. But motherhood is only one part of the caretaking responsibilities that many women today have.

Women may take care of other people who depend on them, including a special needs child, a disabled husband, or an elderly parent.

"The term *caregiver* refers to anyone who provides assistance to someone else who is, to some degree, incapacitated and needs help performing the daily tasks essential to living a normal life. These people may be a husband who has suffered a stroke, a wife with Parkinson's disease, a mother-in-law with cancer, a grandfather with Alzheimer's disease, a loved one with traumatic brain injury, a friend with AIDS, a child with muscular dystrophy, an elder who is very frail."[12]

Fulfilling the role of caregiver can be an arduous task. Maybe you are a caregiver for a debilitated or ill loved one. Your day is given over almost completely to the person who needs your care. You make their meals, give them their medicines, keep them clean and their surroundings sanitary and orderly. Sometimes caretakers can become overwhelmed by the needs of caretaking and can face personal health problems, discouragement, emotional and psychological exhaustion, and depression. For these caregivers, health officials have coined the term "Caretakers Syndrome."

In "The Caregiver Survival Series," Dr. James R. Sherman lists three stages that can evolve from the Caretakers Syndrome, ultimately leading to burnout. "First, frustration stems from not seeing enough progress toward recovery. Next, depression can develop including prolonged periods of helplessness, loss of concentration and control. Ultimately, despair leads to hopelessness and resentment."[13]

The average caretaker is a woman between the ages of fifty and sixty-four. Most are employed, but they often suffer work-related difficulties due to their dual career and care-giving roles. Oftentimes work-related problems cause the caretaker great economic hardships. The more than 65.7 million caregivers make up 29 percent of the adult population of the United States. More than 70 percent of caretakers are caring for aging parents.[14]

LAURA AND TED

Laura[15] was one of 14.9 million Americans caretaking a person suffering with Alzheimer's disease or other dementia.[16] Laura married later in life a man much older than herself. When her husband Ted became a victim of Alzheimer's disease, Laura took care of him full time in their home. As the disease grew worse, Laura's caretaking role became more difficult. For more than four years, Laura cared for Ted and attended to his every need.

"My workload was heavy, and I had to make all the decisions that Ted and I used to make together," Laura remembers. "We lived several hundred miles away from family, and I had to decide whether to sell our house and move us closer to our family or stay in our home. I felt like Ted needed to stay at home where everything was familiar to him. But I also knew that as the disease progressed, I would need more help from my family."

Laura also faced frustrations with Ted's doctors and all the various medications they prescribed for him. "The medications that were supposed to calm him actually produced the opposite effects and agitated him. We could find no medication that helped Ted."

Another frustration for Laura was lack of sleep at night. "When Ted couldn't sleep and felt restlessness at night, I couldn't sleep either. When I was sleep starved, I couldn't do my best work the next day."

During the years of taking care of Ted, Laura stayed close to God. "I depended on my Heavenly Father to guide me in all the decisions I needed to make. When the work and exhaustion overwhelmed me, I prayed that God would send some immediate help—a friend or family member—to take over for a while. When I felt too tired to pray, I knew that others were praying for Ted and me. Their prayers became a great comfort to me."

When Ted died, Laura's caretaking role was far from over. She sold her house and became a full-time caretaker for her elderly mother. She moved into her mother's house and took care of her every need. For more than five years, Laura cared for her fragile mother.

"Fortunately, I had some help from a brother and sister-in-law that lived close by," she remembers. "But my workload and responsibilities weighed heavily on me."

Laura was also getting older herself and found caretaking taxing on her energy. But again, just as with Ted's caretaking, Laura stayed close to God.

"I asked God for strength to get through the day. I also prayed the Scriptures over and over. I found Isaiah 26:3–4 so comforting: 'You will keep in perfect peace / him whose mind is steadfast, / because he trusts in you. Trust in the LORD forever, / for the LORD, the LORD, is the Rock eternal'" (NIV 1984).

Laura, unlike many caretakers today, believed that God gave her permission to rest during her tiring days. "Scripture tells me that God himself rested after he created the world and everything in it, and that Jesus called his disciples together and told them to come with him and get some much needed rest."

Laura found volunteers to sometimes come and stay first with Ted, and later with her mother, when she needed to get away and rest. "I never felt guilty about taking time away from Ted or my mother when the workload and stress overwhelmed me. It was usually only a few days, but it gave me the needed energy to go back to full-time caretaking."

After almost five years of full-time caretaking, one Christmas Day Laura's one-hundred-year-old mother died in her sleep. Between Ted and her mother, Laura had devoted almost a decade to full-time caretaking.

"I depended on God all during that decade," Laura admits. "I prayed that God would show me how to handle each day's demands, help me make the right decisions, and keep me calm when I felt frustrated and stressed. And he did. I found my rest in him."

THE SHARED YOKE

Laura's dependence on God throughout her stressful caretaking days reminds me of Christ's words in Matthew 11:28–30. "Come to me," Jesus said, "all you who are weary and burdened, and I will give you rest. Take my yoke upon you and learn from me, for I am gentle and humble in heart, and you will find rest for your souls. For my yoke is easy and my burden is light."

I had heard the term "yoke" many times, but I wondered what it really meant and why Jesus would use such an interesting metaphor to describe the rest he gives.

I discovered that, in Jesus' day, a yoke paired two oxen together side by side. It was a wooden frame placed on each animal's back with two ropes or wooden loops that slipped around each animal's neck. Pulling together and forward, the yoked oxen could pull carts piled high with heavy loads.

I also learned that sometimes farmers gave the training responsibilities for the younger animals to the older, stronger, more experienced oxen. They yoked the strong ox to the younger, weaker animal. That way, the experienced ox pulled the heavier load so the younger ox's load would be much lighter. This practice helped teach young oxen how to one day become strong and experienced. The yoke made the oxen partners.

Isn't this exactly what Jesus explains to us about helping us carry our heavy loads in life? He calls the weary and burdened to himself, and he offers them his rest for their weary souls. He places our yoke around his own neck and he carries the heaviest part of our load for us. And he promises us, "You will find rest for your souls."

GOD GIVES CARETAKERS PERMISSION TO REST

We, as Christian women, never know when circumstances will call upon us to become part-time or full-time caretakers. But even in that all-consuming role, God gives us his permission to find his rest and his help with our heavy burdens. Not only does he give us permission to rest, he calls us to himself with offered rest.

While most Christian women see caretaking responsibilities as a personal ministry (and it certainly is!), they can often feel psychologically overwhelmed in their responsibilities. They can find psychological relief and rest, however, when they learn from Scripture that they are not alone in their caretaking responsibilities. God is the *primary parent*. He is the primary parent of the woman's healthy children as well as her elderly parents, special-needs sibling, ill husband, and others. As the *ultimate parent*, God controls—and stands *guard*—over his children's lives, directions, and choices.

The whole meaning and concept of the word "Father" indicates the originator, the One who gives care and protection. Jesus told his listeners to address God as "Father." A woman need not think she is alone in her caretaking duties. While she may be essential in her role, she is a *temporary caretaker*, often for a brief period of time. God is the *ultimate parent* of all his children. Knowing this theological truth can help today's Christian women who are primary caretakers experience a peaceful, psychological "soul-rest" in their caretaking roles. A woman can find great rest when she understands that God, not she, is the *ultimate caretaker*. God is the One in complete control of each person's life and future. The whole world is his and he takes responsibility for it and everything in it.

Practical Suggestions

Perhaps you are a single woman, mother, or grandmother with huge responsibilities for children and grandchildren. Or perhaps you are the primary caretaker for a person who is ill, afflicted with Alzheimer's disease or disabilities, or elderly and in need of constant, around-the-clock supervision and care. Know that God gives you his permission to rest even in the midst of a twenty-four-hours-a-day, seven-days-a-week caretaking job. Here are some practical suggestions for finding rest in these trying times of caretaking:

- Sometimes we can feel so alone in our caretaking for others, whether children, grandchildren, or the needy, diseased, and disabled. Know that God is himself the ultimate parent of the person you care for. You are only the temporary caretaker, and, as difficult as that role is, God is the ultimate One who takes responsibility for his child. Women can find psychological rest from this burden and responsibility when they understand that they are only temporary caretakers, and that God himself provides the ultimate responsibility for those he puts in their temporary care.

- Stay close to God through prayer and Scripture. Meditate on those verses in God's Word that bring you peace, such as:
  - Isaiah 26:3–4: "You will keep in perfect peace
    him whose mind is steadfast,
    because he trusts in you.

Trust in the LORD forever,
for the LORD, the LORD, is the Rock eternal." (NIV 1984)

❧ Psalm 34:17–18: "The righteous cry out, and the LORD
hears them;
he delivers them from all their troubles.
The LORD is close to the brokenhearted
and saves those who are crushed in spirit."

❧ Numbers 6:24–26 (A priestly blessing):
"The LORD bless you
and keep you;
the LORD make his face shine upon you
and be gracious to you;
the LORD turn his face toward you
and give you peace."

⌇ Know that God gives you permission to rest your body, mind, emotions, and spirit in him. Sit often in his presence and just listen to him speak to your heart.

⌇ Keep a journal and record your feelings and frustrations. Also write down your moments of joy and inspiration.

⌇ Ask God to help you carry the heavy load, to share your yoke, to give you his promised rest.

⌇ Ask God to send you needed help when the workload becomes overwhelming.

⌇ Rest in the fact that you aren't alone in your caretaking. God is guiding and strengthening you for the weighty responsibilities that you must carry.

⌇ "It's okay to relax your standards—don't put a lot of pressure on yourself to have the 'perfect' house or be the 'perfect' mother. No one expects you to be Superwoman," states APA psychologist Lynn Bufka.[17]

⌇ Find out if your church and/or community offer helpful services for full-time or part-time caretakers and let them help you.

Personal Quiet Time to Rest, Study, Reflect, and Pray

1. Scriptures to read, study, and contemplate:

   Psalm 24:1: "The earth is the LORD's, and everything in it, the world, and all who live in it."

   Psalm 46:7: "The LORD Almighty is with us; the God of Jacob is our fortress."

   Matthew 6:9: "This, then, is how you should pray: *'Our Father* in heaven, / hallowed be your name'" (emphasis added).

   Ephesians 4:4–6: "There is one body and one Spirit, just as you were called to one hope when you were called; one Lord, one faith, one baptism; *one God and Father of all, who is over all and through all and in all*" (emphasis added).

   Psalm 23:1, 3, 4: "The LORD is my *shepherd*, I shall not be in want . . .
   he restores my soul . . .
   for you are with me;
   your rod and your staff,
   they comfort me."
   (NIV 1984)

2. Questions to reflect upon and respond to:

   Ponder your situation in life. Do you have other people who depend on you? How can you find rest in the midst of your responsibilities for others?

   What is the meaning of the "yoke" as Jesus talks about it in Matthew 11:30? How does the "yoke" in Scripture give you

Christ's permission to rest and to allow him to carry the heavy load?

Think about the women you know who are full- or part-time caretakers for children and/or adults. List the numbers of ways you could help them. Offer them your time and energy.

What is meant by the word "fortress"? How is God our "fortress" (Ps. 46:7)?

Psalm 24:1 tells us that the earth, the world, and all its inhabitants belong to the Lord. What message of hope, help, and rest does this Scripture highlight for you? Does it comfort you? How?

3. Prayer suggestions: Pray that God will strengthen you in your child-rearing and/or caretaking role. Pray that God will use you to help other women who carry heavy loads of caretaking.

4. Decisions made (as a result of reading this chapter, studying suggested Scriptures, reflecting upon questions, and praying):

⊗≈ Group Bible Study ≈⊗

1 Read:

Psalm 46:1: "God is our refuge and strength, an ever-present help in trouble."

Philippians 4:7: "And the peace of God, which transcends all understanding, will guard your hearts and your minds in Christ Jesus."

Colossians 3:15: "Let the peace of Christ rule in your hearts, since as members of one body you were called to peace."

Ephesians 2:14: "For he [Christ] himself is our peace."

2. Respond: Questions and comments to consider and respond to as a group:

Discuss how God's peace (which transcends all understanding) is different from the world's peace.

What can your church and community do to help those who carry heavy caretaking loads? List the ways. Take your ideas to your church leaders and offer to help make them happen in your church.

In Psalm 23, the psalmist tells us that the Lord is our "shepherd." What does that image suggest to you? What are the shepherd's responsibilities for the sheep?

Share the resources your church and/or community offer for caretakers. Share these resources with the key leaders in your church and/or community. Make this knowledge available to those who need to know it.

3. Share: Reader will share with group what she has learned from this particular Bible Study and the decisions she has made.

Chapter 10

Resting in Beauty, Harmony, and Peace

Finally, brothers, whatever is true, whatever is noble,
whatever is right, whatever is pure, whatever is lovely,
whatever is admirable—if anything is excellent or
praiseworthy—*think about these things.* (Phil. 4:8 NIV 1984)

✒ *God gives Christian women his permission to rest*
in his created beauty, harmony, and peace. ✒

Women find peaceful rest when they notice, acknowledge,
enjoy, and give thanks for what is beautiful, good, and lovely.
Centering one's thoughts on excellent, right, and pure things and
living in a state of gratitude bring rest.

As I mentioned earlier, scholars believe that when Paul penned his
letter to the Christians in the Roman-controlled city of Philippi, he
was in prison. The ruthless Emperor Nero ruled Rome at the time. If
Paul wrote his letter in AD 62, as believed, the Great Fire of Rome (a
fire blamed on the Christians) and Christian persecution would take
place in Rome only two years later. Paul died in AD 67. The next year,
Nero committed suicide.[1]

No doubt, Paul sat in a deep earthen hole or dark damp dungeon—probably in Rome—with rats and rotting corpses around him.

Yet Paul could still write a letter to the Philippians encouraging them to think on beautiful things, not on the ugly things of the world at that time. He could write, "Rejoice in the Lord always. I will say it again: Rejoice!" (Phil. 4:4). He could also write about "the peace of God, which transcends all understanding" (Phil. 4:7). It seemed that Paul could rest and praise God and "rejoice," even in the most dire circumstances. God offered Paul and Silas that special rest, a peace and rest not dependent on the current situation.

Perhaps Paul sat in prison and remembered his trip to Philippi a decade before. Paul and Silas arrived in Philippi and found no Jewish synagogue there. They found a group of women praying on the Sabbath by the riverside. Lydia had been part of this group. She believed Paul's message about Christ. So grateful to God about her new Lord and Savior, she graciously opened her home to Paul and Silas and the other believers (Acts 16:12–40).

Paul and Silas settled for a while in Philippi, but the city turned against them when Paul exorcised a demon from a slave girl. They beat Paul and Silas, imprisoned them, and put them in stocks. But even in prison, Paul and Silas worshipped God, sang songs, and, no doubt, centered their minds on things true, noble, right, pure, lovely, and admirable.

A SIMPLE WORD STUDY

Why did Paul urge Christians to think about those things that are true, noble, right, pure, lovely, admirable, excellent, and praiseworthy? Perhaps Paul predicted that Nero and the Roman Empire would horribly persecute Christians in a short time. No doubt, he wanted to encourage the Christians to remember Christ, their Savior and Lord, in the midst of horrific circumstances, torture, and death. Over millenniums, the meanings of words can drastically change. But these words mean the same today as they did in ancient times. Let's look more closely at the suggestions he made to the young Christians in Philippi.

TRUE

Whatever is *true*. . . . If something is true, it is factual, sincere, and verifiable. It is in accordance with fact and reality. For example,

- Scripture tells us: "The man who has accepted it [belief in Christ] has certified that God is *truthful* [or *true*]" (John 33 NIV 1984).
- In a beautiful prayer in John 17, Jesus prays, "Now this is eternal life: that they may know you, the only *true* God, and Jesus Christ, whom you have sent" (John 17:3).
- In Revelation 22:6, John writes: "The angel said to me, 'These words are *trustworthy* and *true*. The Lord, the God of the spirits of the prophets, sent his angel to show his servants the things that must soon take place'" (NIV 1984).
- The psalmist writes: "All your words are *true*; all your righteous laws are eternal" (Ps. 119:160).

NOBLE

Whatever is *noble*. . . . We associate the word "noble" with a generous person who possesses fine personal qualities, capability, and high moral principles and ideals. Anything considered noble is of excellent quality.

- Ruth, for instance, was called "a woman of *noble* character" (Ruth 3:11).
- Jesus tells a story about a sower and his seed: "But the seed on good soil stands for those with a *noble* and good heart, who hear the word, retain it, and by persevering produce a crop" (Luke 8:15).
- Paul asks of the Romans: "Does not the potter have the right to make out of the same lump of clay some pottery for *noble* purposes and some for common use?" (Rom. 9:21 NIV 1984).

RIGHT

Whatever is *right*. . . . "Right" means morally good, precise, and true. The opposite of right is wrong or undesirable and bad. For instance,

- God said to Moses and the Children of Israel: "If you listen carefully to the voice of the Lord your God and do what is *right* in his eyes, is you pay attention to his commands and keep all his decrees, I will not bring on you any of the diseases I brought on the Egyptians, for I am the Lord, who heals you" (Exod. 15:26).
- The psalmist writes: "The precepts of the LORD are *right*, giving joy to the heart" (Ps. 19:8).
- "Who is wise? . . . The ways of the LORD are *right*" (Hos. 14:9).
- Paul writes to the Romans: "Do not repay anyone evil for evil. Be careful to do what is *right* in the eyes of everyone" (Rom. 12:17).
- Paul writes to the Thessalonians: "And as for you, brothers, never tire of doing what is *right*" (2 Thes. 3:13 NIV 1984).

Right also meant an important and honored physical position. For instance:

- Scripture tells us that Christ is seated at the *right* hand of God (Mark 16:19, Eph. 1:20, Col. 3:1).

PURE

Whatever is *pure*. . . . When something is pure, it is not adulterated with anything else. It is free of contamination, wholesome, and untainted by immorality.

- "But if we walk in the light, as he is in the light, we have fellowship with one another, and the blood of Jesus, his Son, *purifies* us from all sin" (1 John 1:7).

- "If we confess our sins, he is faithful and just and will forgive us our sins and *purify* us from all unrighteousness" (1 John 1:9).
- When King David asks God to "cleanse me with hyssop, and I will be clean [or *purified*]; / wash me, and I will be whiter than snow [made *pure*]" (Ps. 51:7). (Hyssop, a plant, was used in ancient days for cleansing and in rituals for *purification*.)[2]

LOVELY

Whatever is *lovely*. . . . "Lovely" means exquisitely beautiful, pleasant, delightful. The opposite of lovely is ugly. For example:

- The psalmist writes: "How lovely is your dwelling place, LORD Almighty" (Ps. 84:1).
- The lover in the Songs of Songs describes her beloved: "His mouth is sweetness itself;
  he is altogether *lovely*" (Song of Sol. 5:16).

ADMIRABLE AND PRAISEWORTHY

Whatever is *admirable* and *praiseworthy*. . . . If something is admirable and praiseworthy, it is commendable, honorable, good, and worthwhile. It has merit. The opposite of admirable is deplorable or disgraceful, shameful, and unworthy.

- The psalmist writes: "I will sing *praise* to the God of Jacob" (Ps. 75:9).

EXCELLENT

Whatever is *excellent*. . . . "Excellent" means outstanding and wonderful. Its opposite is inferior. Scripture speaks of excellence in these verses:

- When Paul writes to the Corinthians about the true meaning of love, he tells them: "And now I will show you the most *excellent* way" (1 Cor. 12:31 NIV 1984).
- Titus, a companion of Paul, wrote: "This is a trustworthy saying. And I want you to stress these things, so that those who have trusted in God may be careful to devote themselves to doing what is good. These things are *excellent* and profitable for everyone" (Titus 3:8).

SETTING OUR MINDS ON "HEAVENLY THINGS"

When Paul told Philippi's Christians to think upon those things that were sincere, factual, of excellent quality, good, true, pure and not adulterated, wholesome, moral, lovely, delightful, beautiful, commendable, honorable, outstanding, and worthwhile, he wanted them to "set [their] hearts on things above, where Christ is seated at the right hand of God." He encouraged them, as he also encouraged the Colossians, to "set [their] minds on things above, not on earthly things" (Col. 3:1–2). The "earthly things" around them were political lies, filth, tortures and murders, and situations that produced pain and agony in their lives. As Christians, they swam upstream and against the pagan and violent Roman society, a society laden by scandals and sex and greed. Paul identifies some of the problems and people of his day when he writes, "For, as I have often told you before and now say again even with tears, many live as enemies of the cross of Christ. Their destiny is destruction, their god is their stomach, and their glory is in their shame. Their mind is set on earthly things" But he reminds his readers: "But our citizenship is in heaven" (Phil. 3:18–20).

Living a Christ-honored life in Roman society proved difficult, if not impossible. Perhaps this is why Paul reminds the Philippians that, with Christ's help, "I can do everything through him [Christ] who gives me strength" (Phil. 4:13). Paul knew that only with Christ's strength could the Philippians live honorable lives in the midst of a depraved, pleasure-seeking, and self-indulgent Roman society.

A Message for Women Today

I believe Paul's letters to the Philippians, the Colossians, and other Christians encourage women today to find rest in thankful and peaceful living. God gives us permission to seek rest in the beautiful things of life. I love to spend time in my backyard garden. I fill large pots with an arrangement of brightly colored flowers. I sit in my porch swing and pray, meditate, and thank God for the simple beauty of growing flowers and nature. I listen to the birds chirp, watch an occasion chipmunk scurry across the deck, and delight in the cute antics and playfulness of my three adorable pups. My garden is the perfect place to rest, to center my thoughts on God's gifts of beauty and purity and honor.

But I am discovering that God also equips a woman's mind to dwell on beauty and purity and honor when she is not basking in the sunshine of a flower garden. Paul urges us to think on these lovely and good things when we find ourselves in horrible and painful situations.

Perhaps anyone can think lovely thoughts while sitting in a porch swing surrounded by beauty and flowers. But God has also given his daughters the capacity to center their minds on the beautiful, good, and true things of God in the middle of dirty, violent inner cities, in situations that bring fears and tears, in late-night hospital rooms where a loved one writhes in pain and faces agonizing death, and while working in the midst of children and adults who are impoverished, tired, hungry, and dirty.

Paul also urges the Christians in Philippi to "do everything without complaining or arguing" (Phil. 2:14 NIV 1984). Living in peace and gratitude, noticing God's natural beauty, and dwelling on things lovely and good, will bring rest to a woman's mind, emotions, and spirit. Even if the circumstance she is facing isn't restful, lovely, and good. This type of rest will empower her to choose the battles she needs to

A WOMAN'S RIGHT TO REST

address, and to leave the others unaddressed. Scripture tells us that Christians are "called to peace" when they allow Christ to "rule in [their] hearts" (Col. 3:15).

A Christian woman is called to pray for the warring world around her but to keep her mind centered on God and his purpose and peace.

Practical Suggestions

Do you ever wonder how you can practically apply Paul's advice in Philippians 4:8 to your life when you are in the midst of chaos, turmoil, and/or tragedy? Surely, God has equipped our minds to practice this type of peace and rest in all situations. Otherwise, were it not possible, Scripture would not encourage it. Here are some suggestions that may help you.

- Memorize those Scripture verses that bring to your mind beauty and goodness and loveliness. Repeat them to yourself when you find yourself in trying situations and crises.
- Spend time in beautiful places—flower gardens, parks, by a lake, in the woods. Use these times to notice God's beautiful creations and to thank him.
- Learn to see beauty and goodness in the faces of the people around you.
- Read books that focus on beauty and peace. Step into the pages and see God's beauty through the author's eyes.
- Become an "armchair traveler" by reading books about beautiful places on God's earth.
- Spend time with friends who think about noble and honorable things. Limit your time, if possible, with people who focus on earthly things or who complain, gossip, or grumble.
- Light a candle and think about "light" and its meaning. Ponder how light—even a tiny flame—can dispel darkness.

৯ Read Scriptures about "light" including: Genesis 1:3 (God created light); 2 Samuel 22:29 (The Lord can turn our darkness into light); Psalm 4:6 (The psalmist asks God to "let the light of your face shine upon us"); Psalm 27:1 (The psalmist exclaims with praise that the "LORD is my light and my salvation"); John 8:12 (Jesus is "the light of the world"); Matthew 5:16 ("Let your light shine before men" NIV 1984). When time permits, you might want to do a personal Bible study on the meaning of light as recorded throughout Scripture.

৯ Take a break from the daily dose of bad news and violence that comes to us through television, radio, and newspaper.

৯ Sit still and, in solitude and quiet, mentally list all those things and people you consider blessings from God. You might want to record those blessings and keep them in sight as you go about your busy day.

Personal Quiet Time to Rest, Study, Reflect, and Pray

1. Scriptures: Please read, study, and contemplate the following verses:

Colossians 3:2–3: "Set your minds *on things above, not on earthly things*. For you died, and your life is now hidden with Christ in God."

Philippians 4:8: "Finally, brothers, whatever is true, whatever is noble, whatever is right, whatever is pure, whatever is lovely, whatever is admirable—if anything is excellent or praiseworthy—*think about such things*" (NIV 1984).

Philippians 2:14–15: "Do everything without complaining or arguing, so that you may become blameless and pure, children of God without fault in a crooked and depraved generation, in which you shine like stars in the universe" (NIV 1984).

2. Questions: Please reflect upon and respond to the following:

What does Paul mean when he writes: "For you died, and your life is now hidden with Christ in God"? (Col. 3:3).

Do you have a quiet place of beauty where you can take time to rest and ponder and meditate? If not, will you consider creating a place like this?

What things in your life are true, noble, right, pure, lovely, admirable, excellent, and praiseworthy? Take a moment to thank God for these gifts to you.

3. Prayer suggestions: Pray that God will help you keep your mind on heavenly things as you go about your difficult and busy workday. Thank God for his many blessings to you.

4. Decisions made (as a result of reading this chapter, studying suggested Scriptures, reflecting upon questions, and praying):

Group Bible Study

1. Read:

Philippians 4:8: "Finally, brothers, whatever is true, whatever is noble, whatever is right, whatever is pure, whatever is lovely, whatever is admirable—if anything is excellent or praiseworthy—*think about these things*" (NIV 1984).

2. Respond: Please consider the following questions and respond as a group:

Resting in Beauty, Harmony, and Peace

Ask members in the group to talk about each of the "heavenly things" Paul mentions in Philippians 4:8. Define each word and ask individuals to comment upon each word as it has brought meaning to her life.

3. Share: Reader will share with group what she has learned from this particular Bible study and the decisions she has made.

THE REST OF SELECTED MEMORIES

I have been *reminded* of your sincere faith,
which first lived in your grandmother
Lois and in your mother Eunice and, I am
persuaded, now lives in you also. (2 Tim. 1:5)

ﾞ *God gives Christian women his permission*
to rest in pleasant memories. ﾞ

M y son, Christian, on his second birthday, ran as fast as he could
run directly into the street during heavy 5:00 afternoon traffic.
When the traffic light in front of our home turned green, hundreds
of cars raced along the four lanes of highway going sixty-five miles
per hour.

We had bought our "little house on the freeway" when Timothy
and I moved to Louisville, Kentucky, and Timothy began teaching at
the Southern Baptist Theological Seminary. The tiny two-story old
house sat on the edge of the highway. I became pregnant and gave birth
to both our children while we lived in that house. We had no air con-
ditioning, no washer or dryer, and only one small upstairs bathroom.
But we appreciated that house. We had little money and spent most

everything we earned paying back student loans from seven years of graduate school. It was the only place we could afford at that time.

Our neighbors next door had invited us and a few others to a cook-out to celebrate Christian's birthday. Our two-year-old was pure energy. We could hardly keep up with him. He was mischievous and quick, and we never took our eyes off him. But, on this afternoon, when we blinked, Christian took off toward the highway. Someone screamed, and Timothy raced after Christian. I had never seen my husband run as fast. Christian ran into the middle of the highway with Timothy racing several feet behind him. It could have meant instant death for Christian, but seconds before he stepped into the street, the green light changed to red, and the cars stopped. Timothy scooped up Christian in his arms, took a few deep breaths of relief, and took him into the house.

The whole scene lasted only a few seconds. But it was terrifying. That night I couldn't sleep. I kept envisioning my little son lying dead on the street in the midst of racing cars. I replayed the scene over and over in my mind. I concentrated on how very close we came to losing Christian that afternoon.

I'll admit that, for many years, I replayed that near-tragedy in my mind. Again and again and again. I told my family and friends about every detail of it. The frightening memory interrupted my sleep. It upset my stomach. I found concentration difficult.

The next day, I bought a strong chain link fence and had it placed around our entire yard. But that still didn't ease my thoughts and worries. I finally put the house up for sale and moved to a house on a *cul de sac*. We could barely afford the move and the house, but I felt we had no choice. I had to find some relief to my growing fears about the highway in front of our house.

WHAT I NOW KNOW THAT I DIDN'T KNOW THEN

I wish I had known then what I know now in my later years of life. God gives us, his daughters, the mental capability to control our fearful and tragic thoughts. In that we can find great rest from agonizing memories that plague us, hurt our health, and dampen our joy.

Painful memories can negatively engage our mind and constantly interrupt our daily lives. A memory is an interesting mystery. When we remember an event, we don't just "think about it again." We actually, in our minds and hearts, "relive" the event. We then go through the same horrific and frightening feelings we experienced when we first witnessed the troubling event. Painful memories can keep us from resting, sleeping, and relating with joy to those we love. They can also hinder us in our personal ministries to others.

But the good news is—we don't have to allow negative and painful memories to pitch a tent and live in our minds. We can decide to remember them no more! We can put them out of our head and heart! We can find freedom from them! And we can choose to think on those lovely and pure virtues Paul tells us about in his letter to the Philippians (as we saw in the previous chapter).

Consider this: if our human mind didn't possess the God-endowed capability to think admirable and praiseworthy thoughts (instead of focusing on unpleasant thoughts), then Paul's advice to the Philippians might be considered cruel. He would be asking the Philippians to do something they were not capable of doing. Instead, by his telling them to think on lovely things, he acknowledged to those Philippian Christ-believers that they could, indeed, focus their minds and hearts on "heavenly things" and delete from their minds those "earthly things."

More Good News

Paul gives us a good example of controlling our thoughts when he recounts his own sordid and violent past. Listen to his words to young Timothy: "I thank Christ Jesus our Lord, who has given me strength, that he considered me faithful, appointing me to his service." Then Paul shares a bit of his past with the young man: "Even though I was once a blasphemer and a persecutor and a violent man, I was shown mercy because I acted in ignorance and unbelief." Paul then states the reason he can put his wicked past behind him. "The grace of our Lord was poured out on me abundantly, along with the faith and love that are in Christ Jesus" (1 Tim. 1:12–14 NIV 1984). Paul then adds to his confession: "Christ Jesus came into the world to save sinners—of whom I am the worst" (1 Tim. 1:15).

Paul described himself as a *blasphemer*—one who swears, curses, and takes the Lord God's name in vain. A blasphemer speaks irreverently about God. He is known as an "evil-speaker." Paul admits he was also a *persecutor*—a person who harasses and treats with hostility those with different religious or political beliefs or those belonging to another race. Paul was actually a "Christian-killer." He hunted down Christians like a hound with a passion for blood. How interesting that God chose Saul, the terrorist, to become Paul, the Christ-follower and evangelist!

How did Paul overcome the memories of his past life to become a missionary that could encourage the Philippians to think about things that are true, noble, right, pure, lovely, admirable, excellent, and praiseworthy?

Paul tells us his secret in Philippians 3:13–14: "*Forgetting what is behind and straining toward what is ahead*, I press toward the goal to win the prize for which God has called me heavenward in Christ Jesus."

He willed his mind to "forget" the wicked memories of his past, all those things he had put behind him. When Paul decided to "forget," he didn't "lose facts from his mind." The human brain is an incredible organ. It keeps detailed records of our wickedness and our trials and has the ability to bring them vividly to our minds at all times of the day or night. When Paul decided to "forget" the horrible memories of his earlier life, he chose "to remember them no more." In other words, when a painful memory came to mind, he immediately refused to think about or dwell on those things he had put behind him. He focused instead on his current mission and passion—Jesus Christ—and he "strained" toward his heavenward goal and prize.

The writer of Hebrews also encourages Christians to "throw off everything that hinders and the sin that so easily entangles" (Heb. 12:1). Why? So that we can "run with perseverance the race marked out for us" (Heb. 12:1). How do we do that? We "fix our eyes on Jesus, the author and perfecter of our faith" (Heb. 12:2 NIV 1984).

OUR GIFT OF MEMORY

God himself has given women the beautiful gift of memory. Women can remember (and thus re-experience) a wonderful childhood event, a delightful moment from her wedding, a child's greatly anticipated birth, and other times in her life that bring joy to her heart and a smile to her lips.

Often, however, a woman's mind may remember (and thus re-experience) an unpleasant moment: a friend's hateful words, a despairing situation, a wrong decision she made long ago. Sometimes the memory might be a terrible and painful one—a husband's unexpected death, a fatal car crash, a child's devastating illness. Painful memories can also torment a woman's mind when an event *almost happened*—a child running out in front of a truck and *almost getting hit*, an elderly parent's falling and *almost hitting her head*, and so on. Thank God that he gives us the ability to put those negative memories behind us and get on with the abundant life he gives his daughters.

I don't allow myself to remember the day Christian ran out into the highway and could have been instantly killed. I have thought about it briefly today so that I can share it with you. But now I can choose to put that awful memory behind me, to dwell on it no more, to forget it, and to remember it no more. God gives his daughters the gift of "selected memories." Whenever I am tempted to think about my son's second birthday and about the tragedy that almost happened to him, I instead focus my thoughts on the fine man and husband he has become, about his writing abilities, about his teaching abilities, and about how God is using him today to bring others closer to Christ. Those are the things I want to dwell on and thank God for.

Practical Suggestions

- Decide to stop thinking about or dwelling on painful memories. Know that God has given you the ability to put them behind you and remember them no more.

- Remove from your home and/or sight those things that tempt you to remember painful or negative events in your past. For instance, replace the photos in your photograph album that bring you inner pain or sad memories and replace them with photos that bring special edifying thoughts and memories.

- Spend more time with friends who help recall those happy memories of the past. Spend less time with those people who won't allow you to forget unpleasant memories and who waste precious time rehashing them.

- Take time each day to sit quietly, remember good memories, and thank God for the ways he has blessed your life.

- Record in a journal all the wonderful times of your life and all the special people who have brought you joy, encouragement, and comfort. Whenever you are tempted to remember a painful memory, read the joyful memories you have penned in your journal.

- Know that we often associate a painful memory with a particular place. Stay away, if possible, from those places that turn your mind back to unpleasant memories.

- When a sad and upsetting memory comes to mind, instantly dispel it. Say aloud: "I have chosen not to think about that memory or event." Pray that God will strengthen you in your resolve to put that memory behind you. Replace it with a memory that brings you joy and rest.

Personal Quiet Time to Rest, Study, Reflect, and Pray

1. Scripture: Please read, study, and contemplate:

   Philippians 3:13–14: *"Forgetting what is behind and straining toward what is ahead*, I press toward the goal to win the prize for which God has called me heavenward in Christ Jesus."

2. Questions: Please reflect upon and respond to the following:

   What is meant by the phrase "forgetting what is behind?" What does this phrase mean personally to you at this time in your life?

   What does Paul mean when he uses the term "straining toward what is ahead"?

   What is the "prize" for pursuing God and his kingdom work?

3. Prayer suggestions: Pray that God will strengthen you and help you control your negative thoughts—those memories most painful to your mind—and give you rest from them. Pray that God will teach you how to reach out to other Christian women who need to forget what is behind and strain toward what is ahead.

4. Decisions made (as a result of reading this chapter, studying suggested Scriptures, reflecting upon questions, and praying):

✑ Group Bible Study ✑

1. Read:

   Hebrews 12:1–2: "Let us throw off everything that hinders and the sin that so easily entangles. And *let us run with perseverance the race marked out for us, fixing our eyes on Jesus,* the pioneer and perfecter of our faith."

2. Respond: Please consider the following questions and respond as a group:

   Ask members of the group to tell how each one has learned to "fix [her] eyes on Jesus," and how this practice has changed her life.

   What does the writer of Hebrews mean when he encourages his readers to "run with perseverance the race marked out for us"? What is "the race," and how can we, God's daughters, best "run it"?

3. Share: Reader will share with group what she has learned from this particular Bible study and the decisions she has made.

Chapter 12

RESTING IN FRIENDSHIP

I no longer call you servants, . . . instead, I have called you *friends*, for everything that I learned from my Father I have made known to you. (John 15:15)

✿ *God gives Christian women his permission to rest in his friendship and in friendships with others.* ✿

E very time I hear this beautiful and well-known story of the deep friendship and devotion of two brothers, I am touched in a new way. The true story took place in the fifteenth century in a tiny village near Nuremberg. Eighteen children filled Albrecht Durer the Elder's home. Two of his children Albrecht and Albert each had been born with incredible artistic gifts and each yearned to study at the Academy in Nuremberg. But the family had no money to send either son to the Academy.

One day Albrecht and Albert came to a decision. One brother would go into the mines and do hard manual labor and pay for the other brother's education at the Academy. Then, after that brother graduated, the other brother would do the same for him. They tossed a coin, and Albrecht won the first Academy education.

Albrecht received a first-class education at the Academy while Albert worked four long hard years in the dangerous mines to finance it. At the end of four years, the Durer family held a festive dinner to celebrate Albrecht's artistic success and triumphant homecoming. After the meal, music, and laughter, Albrecht stood up and told his brother: "And now, Albert, it is your turn to pursue your artistic dream and go to the Academy, and I will take care of you financially." All eyes turned to Albert as he wiped tears from his face. Albrecht noticed his brother's hands. Each finger showed scars of healed broken bones. Hard labor, injury, and arthritis had destroyed Albert's hands. "No, brother," Albert said. "I cannot go to Nuremberg. It is too late for me. Look at my hands. They can no longer hold a brush or pen."

Albrecht painstakingly drew his brother's twisted worn hands as they folded together in prayer. He named his powerful drawing "Hands." "The Praying Hands" became a symbol of selflessness and friendship all over the world. It remains one of Albrecht Durer's most beloved works of art.[1]

Our Friendship with God through Christ

Friendships come to the Christian in two ways. God has brought his daughters into a very close relationship with him through the sacrifice of his Son, Jesus the Christ. We have friendship and peaceful rest with God because he has saved us and justified us (Rom. 5:1) through Christ. He has transformed us and has shaped our heart to love and be loved by him and by others. He has brought to us his precious reconciliation and reunion.

"Greater love has no one than this," Jesus said "that he lay down his life for his friends. You are my friends if you do what I command. I no longer call you servants. . . . Instead, I have called you friends, for everything that I learned from my Father I have made known to you" (John 15:13–15 NIV 1984).

God, through Christ, has chosen us as his friends. He calls us to "go and bear fruit—fruit that will last" (John 15:16).

People Need Each Other!

People need the Lord's friendship! I cannot imagine life without God the Father! People also need each other. I cannot imagine life without good friends!

From the beginning of creation, God created people to need each other. Scripture tells us, "And the LORD God said, 'It is not good that the man should be alone; I will make him an help meet for him'" (Gen. 2:18 ERV). God created Eve to be Adam's companion, and both humans enjoyed wonderful and close companionship with God.

Rest and peace come through God's gifts to us—friends and companions. Jesus himself found great rest when he traveled to the home of his friends, Lazarus, Mary, and Martha (Luke 10:38–41). The three siblings lived in Bethany, near Jerusalem. We learn from Luke that Martha exercised her gift of hospitality through the meals she cooked and served Jesus and his companions. (Sometimes the workload got the best of Martha, however. We see in Luke 10:40 that Martha had a bit of a temper!) Mary, on the other hand, welcomed Jesus into their home with her heart. Like a sponge, she listened to his every word and teaching and soaked it all up while sitting at his feet. John tells us that Jesus visited the Bethany home of his friends six days before his last Passover. At that point, Jesus knew his time on earth was brief. He faced with dread his crucifixion in Jerusalem during the time of Passover. Perhaps he needed the comfort of his friends before he made his last journey to Jerusalem.

Martha prepared a meal for Jesus and his companions and served them. She graciously gave the dinner party to honor Jesus. But John tells us that Mary did something quite unusual that evening as the guests reclined at the table to eat. Mary took a pint of expensive perfume ("pure nard") and poured it on Jesus' feet. Then she wiped his feet with her hair. John records that the perfumed fragrance spread throughout the room. What an interesting thing for Mary to do! What was its significance?

Jesus himself explains the reason for Mary's selfless act of love. Judas verbally objected to Mary's pouring expensive perfume on Jesus' feet. (In ancient days, nard came from northern India and the aromatic oil was extremely expensive. We aren't told where Mary bought or received the nard, but it was hers to give Jesus as a gift.) Judas asked, "Why wasn't this perfume sold and the money given to the poor? It was worth a year's wages" (John 12:5). (John tells his readers that Judas, the one who betrayed Jesus, was a thief and wanted the money for himself [John 12:6].)

"Leave her alone," Jesus told Judas. And then Jesus helps us to understand the purpose of Mary's action. "It was intended that she should save this perfume for the day of my burial. You will always have the poor among you, but you will not always have me" (John 12:7–8). Mary must have instinctively known this would be the final time she sat at Jesus' feet and listened to him teach. She was saying "goodbye" in her own remarkable way.

Mary, Martha, and Lazarus comforted Jesus, fed him, and gave him a place to rest when he most needed encouragement and strength and friendship. And Jesus also comforted Mary and Martha when they most needed it. Jesus had traveled to Bethany after Lazarus died (John 11). He comforted Martha with a talk about resurrection theology (John 11:21–27). His words of promise and hope gave Martha a restful heart. Mary, however, just needed someone to cry with her. When she saw Jesus, she simply fell at his feet. And with her, "Jesus wept" (John 11:35). With his tears, Jesus gave Mary a rested heart.

Mary, Martha, Lazarus, and Jesus had a special friendship. We can learn both how to be a friend to others in need and how to allow others to be a friend to us when we need comfort and strength. Through his example, Jesus teaches Christians today about friendship and the need we have for companionship.

OTHER FRIENDS IN SCRIPTURE

Scripture tells us about other friends who loved and helped each other.

- David and Saul's son Jonathan became good friends (1 Sam. 18:1–4).
- Naomi and Ruth proved much more than mother-in-law and daughter-in-law to each other. They genuinely loved and cared for each other (Ruth 1:1–19).
- Daniel had companions—Hananiah, Mishael, and Azariah—as he sought to live for God in pagan Babylon under Nebuchadnezzar's reign (Dan. 1:6–11). And when Nebuchadnezzar threw into the fiery furnace the Jews who refused to worship him as a god, Shadrach, Meshach, and Abednego had the companionship of each other (Dan. 3:13–30). The three men also had the companionship of another as they walked around in the fire, unbound and unharmed. "Look!" shouted King Nebuchadnezzar, "I see four men walking around in the fire" (Dan. 3:25).
- Paul frequently depended on his friends to minister to him in strange cities and to help him establish new churches in his missionary travels. (Many of Paul's friends are listed in Acts and in his letters to the churches.)
- Selfless Tabitha (sometimes called Dorcas) ministered to many of her poor and widow friends in Joppa. When she died, her friends gathered around her, "crying and showing [Peter] the robes and other clothing that Dorcas had made while she was still with them" (Acts 9:36–43).

To have a friend and to be a friend in biblical days proved a great gift and honor. The writer of Proverbs stated,

A man of many companions [false friends] may come to ruin,
but there is a friend who sticks closer than a brother.
(Prov. 18:24 NIV 1984)

The writer also stated, "A friend loves at all times" (Prov. 17:17). The
writer of Ecclesiastes spoke about the practical reason for having faithful friends:

Two are better than one . . .
If one falls down,
his friend can help him up.
But pity the man who falls
and has no one to help him up!
(Eccles. 4:9–10 NIV 1984)

A SPECIAL GIFT TO WOMEN

While men need friends, new studies are showing that women need
friends to "shape who we are and who we are yet to be." One recent
study showed that women with friends are less likely "to develop physical impairments as they age" and more likely "to be leading a joyful
life." A lack of close friends proved as "detrimental to your health as
smoking or carrying extra weight."[2]

Women spending time together, scientists are discovering, "can
actually counteract the kind of stomach-quivering stress most of us
experience on a daily basis. A landmark UCLA study suggests that
women respond to stress with a cascade of brain chemicals that cause
us to make and maintain friendships with other women." The hormone *oxytocin* (released within a woman as part of the stress response)
"buffers the fight or flight response and encourages her to tend children and gather with other women instead." When she engages in
this "tending and befriending," "studies suggest that more *oxytocin* is
released, which further counters stress and produces a calming effect."
The studies show that men do not experience this physical response.[3]

Friendship among women is so essential, researcher and author Dr. Ruthellen Josselson, cautions busy women who might neglect their friends, "Every time we get overly busy with work and family, the first thing we do is let go of friendship with other women. . . . That's really a mistake," she writes, "because women are such a source of strength to each other. We nurture one another. And we need to have unpressured space in which we can do the special kind of talk that women do when they're with other women. It's a very healing experience."[4]

One study shows that when women have children, they most often drastically reduce the time they spend with their friends "barely five hours each week, down from 14 hours a week before having a child."[5]

Another study shows that women need each other for emotional support and identity. When women get together and bond, they become part of an entire emotional support system.

Studies at Ohio State and Carnegie Mellon University have shown that "people who report strong social supports have more robust immune systems and are less likely to succumb to infectious disease."[6]

Friendships among women can produce both psychological benefits as well as physical gains.

"Psychologically, women gain self-esteem, validation, and happiness" from friendships with other women. "Female friends can boost each other's self-worth through compliments, honest opinions, and suggestions. In times of trouble, females seek one another out to know that their feelings . . . are normal and healthy. From these interactions, female friends bring away an increase sense of happiness and fulfillment."[7]

Studies show that when women spend time with good friends who validate them, they experience "a lowering of heart rate, blood pressure, stress . . . and the immune and digestive systems work more efficiently."[8]

Some research shows that women have fewer friends today than just a few years ago. Some believe women spend time with Internet friends through Facebook (and other social media) than they do in real life. Friends need to spend more face-to-face time together. Researcher Julianne Holt-Lunstad states, "People who have more [friends], or more complex, social resources vs. people who have less, have higher rates of survival."[9]

"Women are keepers of each other's secrets, boosters of one another's wavering confidence, co-conspirators in life's adventures. Through laughter, tears and an inexhaustible river of talk, they keep each other well, and make each other better," writes Melissa Healy in a *Los Angeles Times* article.[10]

Close friendships help women overcome loneliness. "Women who report loneliness die earlier, get sick more often and weather transitions with greater physical wear and tear than those who say they have a support network of friends or family." Dr. James J. Lynch, a psychologist who works with cardiac rehabilitation patients, writes, "Loneliness is simply one of the principal causes of premature death in this country."[11]

We are learning, with each new study, how God made women to be relational. He created them to need and to enjoy friends. Women find great comfort, encouragement, and security in their friendships. God himself offers his daughters great rest, as well as great physical and emotional benefits, in encouraging them to spend time with friends who are trustworthy, dedicated Christians and loyal companions. Jesus certainly knew the strength, support, comfort, and rest brought about by good friends. And he gives women today permission to rest in their friendships and, in return, to give the gift of rest to their friends.

Practical Suggestions

If you want to find rest in God's gift of friendship and companionship, here are some suggestions.

- ⚜ Spend face-to-face time with those you call "friends," the women who uplift, encourage, and genuinely love you. Be a true friend to them.

၆ Love the friends God has sent you. Listen to them with your ears and your heart when they speak. Regard them as a treasure in your life and a gift from God to you.

၆ Rejoice and be happy with your friends when they accomplish great things. Cry and mourn with them when they experience great loss. Be ready to offer love, support, encouragement, and practical help when they need it.

၆ Be kind and considerate to your friends. Pray for them. Remember the occasions that are special to them: birthdays, anniversaries, special remembrances, and the like. Stay in touch with your friends, whether by email, phone, letters, cards, or chats over coffee.

Personal Quiet Time to Rest, Study, Reflect, and Pray

1. Scriptures: Please read, study, and contemplate the following:

Matthew 26:36–37: "Then Jesus went with his disciples to a place called Gethsemane, and he said to them, 'Sit here while I go over there and pray.' He took Peter and the two sons of Zebedee [James and John] along with him." (Jesus had good friends who sometimes let him down when he most needed them. Forgiveness is an essential part of maintaining good friendships.)

Luke 10:1: "After this the Lord appointed seventy-two others and sent them *two by two* ahead of him to every town and place where he was about to go." (How comforting to travel with a companion instead of traveling alone. Jesus sent his missionaries out in pairs for a reason.)

John 15:13–14: "Greater love has no one than this, that he lay down his life for his friends. You are my friends" (NIV 1984).

(Christ has given us this wonderful gift of his friendship. Enjoy it. Find rest in it.)

2. Questions: Please reflect upon and respond to the following:

How did Peter and James and John disappoint Jesus in Matthew 26:36? How did Jesus respond to them? What can we learn from this example?

Why do you believe Jesus sent out the appointed 72 in pairs?

Ponder this statement and then record your thoughts: Women can find comfort, rest, and great security when they share their problems, concerns, and sorrows with trusted Christian friends. Strength often comes through sharing. Comforting rest comes when a woman finds a friend who is trustworthy, compassionate, caring and concerned—a friend she never seeks to impress with social status, accomplishments, or wealth of possessions. A friend is someone who accepts and loves without condition, and in all kinds of situations—joy and crisis.

How can you find more time to spend with your friends? Why should you seek more time for friends?

3. Prayer suggestions: Pray that God will give you rest and joy through the friends he provides you. Pray for your friends, that God will bless and keep them and will give them rest.

4. Decisions made (as a result of reading this chapter, studying suggested Scriptures, reflecting upon questions, and praying):

⇜ Group Bible Study ⇝

1. Read:

   Exodus 33:11: "The LORD would speak to Moses face to face, as a man speaks with his friend" (NIV 1984).

   Mark 1:14–15: "After John was put in prison, Jesus went into Galilee, proclaiming the good news of God. 'The time has come,' he said. 'The kingdom of God has come near. Repent and believe the good news!'" (Read also Mark 1:16–20.)

   John 11:5: "Jesus loved Martha and her sister and Lazarus."

2. Respond: Please consider the following questions and comments and respond as a group:

   Describe the friendship God shared with Moses. How was it unique?

   Why do you think Jesus chose twelve friends to support and help him in his new ministry? Name the disciples he chose. Did they befriend Jesus and/or did they let him down?

   Describe the comforting and restful friendship Jesus shared with Martha, Mary, and Lazarus. What special qualities did their friendships have?

   In his greatest sorrow, Jesus went to Gethsemane to pray. He purposely took with him his three closest friends: Peter, James, and John (Matt. 26:36–37). He found rest in the fact that *he thought* they would pray for him as he prayed. Describe what happened as recorded in Scripture.

3. Share: Reader will share with group what she has learned from this particular Bible study and the decisions she has made.

Chapter 13

Resting in Times of Crisis

The righteous cry out, and *the Lord hears them;*
he delivers them from all their troubles.
The *Lord* is close to the *brokenhearted*
and saves those who are *crushed in spirit.*
(Ps. 34:17–18)

꩜ *God gives Christian women his permission to
rest in him during crisis, pain, and loss.* ꩜

This is the type of biblical rest God gives to his daughters when they fall into crisis—that is, the sudden terminal disease or death of a loved one, a child's serious sickness or life-threatening injury, a cancer diagnosis, a divorce, a husband's prison sentence, the anticipation of one's own death, and other such events. Through his Holy Spirit, God supports, strengthens, and carries the woman in crisis and helps her through the dark and difficult days.

I find great inspiration whenever I read the popular "Footprints Prayer." A woman walks along a sandy beach with the Lord. She sees his footprints in the sand beside her own footprints when things are going well in her life. But, in times of crisis, she notices that Christ's footprints are missing. She believes he has left her at the time she most needs him. The Lord then tells her that she saw only one set of footprints in her brokenhearted times because he carried her.[1]

The prayer is a beautiful reminder that God carries us through our times of pain and sorrow, those "crushed in spirit" times every woman experiences in her life.

Jesus himself cried out to the Father and sought comfort and rest in his time of greatest anguish. He prayed on the Mount of Olives shortly before his arrest: "Father, if you are willing, take this cup from me; yet not my will, but yours be done" (Luke 22:42). So powerfully did Jesus pray, so deep was his agony, Luke the physician states that "his sweat was like drops of blood falling to the ground" (Luke 22:44).

God sent an angel from heaven to Jesus to give him comfort and strength (Luke 22:43).

NATURAL CRISES

A crisis is a time when we might experience intense difficulty, trouble, or danger. Oftentimes a crisis triggers a major turning point in our lives. Some crises come to us through nature. The influenza pandemic (some call it the Spanish flu) in 1918–1919, killed between thirty-five and seventy-five million people in the world. This flu became known as the worst natural disaster to happen in the last thousand years.[2]

Earth has been hit by earthquakes that killed people and destroyed property as well as droughts, floods, tidal waves and tsunami, landslides, diseases, cyclones, tornadoes, hurricanes, volcanoes, famine, wildfires, storms, and blizzards. As humans, we are at the mercy of nature, the uncontrollable force that can instantly interrupt our lives and cause fear and tragedy.

HUMAN-CAUSED CRISES

Some worldwide, life-changing crises are caused by humans. I lived in Chelsea, Massachusetts, in the 1970s when teenagers set a fire in an old tire factory that burned through and destroyed most of the city. It was a frightening experience. I lived in Switzerland the year (1986) that Chernobyl exploded, killed people, and caused worldwide anxiety about possible radiation poisoning. The accident came from a flawed reactor design operated by inadequately trained personnel.[3]

Human beings cause wars. Consider the devastation and loss of life caused by World War I (some estimate casualties of thirty-seven million people)[4] and World War II (casualties number more than forty-eight million people).[5] Each death forever changed the course of world history.

And who will ever forget the terrorists who hijacked U.S. planes and purposely crashed them into New York's World Trade Center, and the Washington, DC, Pentagon. The United States suffered a great loss of lives and property from these planned and coordinated suicide attacks by Islamist militant group al Qaeda. Almost three thousand people died in those attacks.

Personal Crises

As women, we know all too well how natural crises and human-caused crises can interrupt our lives at any unexpected season and cause injury, pain, and death to the world's populace. We also know about personal crises that send us into shock and tears and grief.

I remember my dad's heart surgery at a hospital in Chattanooga, Tennessee, in 1999. The surgery went well, and Daddy prepared to go home after five days recovering in the hospital. Then came a medical mistake that put him flat on his back, on a respirator, and in great pain for the next nine months. He never recovered from the medical mistake. He died two weeks before Christmas, 1999.

Two years ago, a dear friend of our family received news that his grown son had been shot to death at the restaurant where he worked.

Several years ago, my good friend's college-aged daughter was killed instantly in a car accident. The next week, her mother died.

My friend had to plan and attend two funerals the same week—her daughter's and her mother's.

Personal crises enter all our lives, and we deal with them the best we can. But, as Christian women, we have a source of great help when we face a personal crisis. We have our Heavenly Father, the One who is all-powerful and all-loving. We can go to him and depend on him to give us peaceful rest even in the midst of personal suffering and crisis.

Our Father promises to hear us when we cry out to him and stay close to us when our hearts are broken and our spirits are crushed. He calls us to cast our cares on him and allow him to sustain us through our crises. He promises to give us his loving presence when we go through times of shock, pain, suffering, and loss. And he promises us rest during those times we hurt too bad to even pray. We can know, without a doubt, we have a loving Heavenly Father who carries us in his arms when we can no longer walk by ourselves. "My presence will go with you," he promises, "And I will give you *rest*" (Ex. 33:14). Just knowing that God's presence surrounds us gives us incredible rest that when we do face an unexpected and painful crisis, he is there with us.

GOD IS THE SOURCE OF OUR STRENGTH

I first met my good friend Deborah Cooper when she drove from Louisville, Kentucky, to Birmingham, Alabama, to attend one of our Boot Camp for Christian Writers seminars.[6] I immediately bonded in friendship with this lovely Christian woman who loves to write as much as I do. Soft-spoken, kind, and Christ-devoted, Deborah shared with me the crisis that happened in her family more than a dozen years ago. Deborah's husband Raymond worked in highly technical and specialized fields. In 1999, doctors diagnosed him with a rare type of Parkinson's disease called supranuclear palsy. This brain disorder causes serious problems with walking, balance, and eye movements. As the incurable disease progresses, the brain cells that control movement deteriorate and symptoms worsen.[7] Their sons were eleven and fourteen at the time. Raymond had to give up his job, and Deborah took over all aspects of running their home: paying the bills and taxes, maintaining the car and home, frugally running the household and juggling her husband's care while continuing to maintain the two boys' high academic program of home education and their full schedule of speech and debate tournaments on a local, regional, and national level.

"My day-to-day schedule revolves around mealtimes," Deborah told me. "Just this week we found out Ray can no longer go to the Senior Center several hours a day. He can no longer take care of his personal needs or feed himself, two things the Senior Center required for its members. He now struggles even more to walk due to the growing weakness in his lower limbs. And he runs completely out of stamina without warning."

Before, while Ray visited the Senior Center, Deborah could do chores, run errands, and rest. But now, because of his worsening condition, no center nearby could minister to his specific needs.

"Ray also suffers from dementia, and that interferes with good judgment and decision-making. For instance, he thinks he can walk without his walker. He tries to stand up without it and ends up on the floor, baffled at this newly developed inability to walk."

How does Deborah cope with her husband's deteriorating health, the day-to-day crises that result from his illness, and the exhaustion that comes to her as a full-time caretaker? How does she find peace and rest when she knows her husband's health will continue to decline?

"In my times of desperation," she says, "I dig deeply into the Bible and earnestly pray. Even now, as we are entering the moderate to late stages of my husband's disease, I see the same pattern prevail: I pray and I obey. I do not have a formula for my devotional time, although I see a tapestry loosely interwoven with worship, prayer, meditation on scripture, intercessory prayer, and listening to the Lord."

Deborah has also found rest in writing and journaling. "During this time, I may also journal and write poetry. But I think the most important aspect of my relationship with the Lord is when I listen, rest in his love, and literally hear his still, small voice directing my steps. Just this week, I heard these words: 'The body fades; the soul is eternal. Tend to the body, take care of the soul.'"

Deborah has learned to adapt to her crisis situation. Her grown son David stays with Ray while Deborah attends a weekly class at church. "I engage in my tasks, but when Ray wants or needs something, I stop my activities. I have learned, when his eyes are bright, to allow our love to flow and to share our life stories. It is then that I thank him for specific things he has done—especially his loving the Lord and his family. We share these rare deep moments together and we are grateful for this special time to reminisce."

She also admits, "I have been given a huge dose of perseverance to plod forward and endure the hardships. I also find great pleasure in creating a home, special occasions, and hospitality. But I am continually 'morphing' and either adding a new skill or letting go of a 'tradition' because it interferes with creating the canvas of love that exists in our home right now. It's all about the 'now.' The moment. That is where Ray lives. I choose to join him there."

Deborah admits that dealing with their family's crisis and Ray's disease is "definitely not for the faint of heart. Cowards do not become caregivers," she says. "I've come to realize that God spectacularly shows himself strong in our suffering. I don't make announcements or expect pats on the back. I just arise daily and serve. I've found that the Lord actually serves through me now . . . and it's a joy to serve and do the tiniest, most mundane chores."

Deborah admits that she yearns for a life "that has a natural rhythm, a predictable schedule." "The only 'real' constant I have is my time with the Lord in the middle of the night," she says. "I know he'll fill my cup and give me the strength to go on. Sometimes I am so weary. I sing hymns or choruses softly to God, and he fills my soul with his presence. I have no set devotional pattern except to 'show up' for our time together. Over the years, God and I have developed such a deep relationship. I know he is my anchor and will keep me stable through the day. I've found a contentment and restful peace in focusing on 'the moment.' My worship has also become focusing on the task at hand—the folding of socks, taking out the garbage, driving to doctors' appointments."

Over the past couple of nights, Ray has gotten out of bed during the night and fallen to the floor. Her son David comes to her home, picks Ray up, and settles him back into bed.

As Ray's disease progresses, Deborah's workload increases. Ray now needs assistance in "dressing, showering, remembering his medications, and being aware that he may need a spoon along with his knife and fork. Sometimes I must cut his meat for him. At breakfast this morning, we came up with the idea of putting a tray from the table to his chest, to catch the ever-increasing crumbs that fall out of his mouth. I can honestly say, however, that what used to repulse me no longer does. Love covers. Love serves. Love gives . . . whatever is needed, and love adapts. I am far from perfect. I cry before the Lord to help me—to be merciful toward me. And I see his hand of mercy and favor."

God has given Deborah rest in the crisis. "I no longer worry," she tells me. "I know God supplies all my needs according to his riches in Christ Jesus. He has over and over again proven himself strong on my behalf. That does not preclude me from crying out in desperation, though. I know he hears my cries. . . . He moves heaven and earth for his children."

What Scriptures bring Deborah the most rest and comfort? Philippians 2:3–9, Romans 8:14–39 (especially vv. 14–17), Mark 15:21.

"Mark 15:21 has become especially dear to me," Deborah admits, "because I spent so many years with the 'warped' idea that I had to 'do it myself.' When we obey Christ, we become like him. When he tells us that we have to carry our cross, sometimes it becomes too heavy for us and others are compelled by the love of Christ to help. And even Christ needed help to carry his cross!"

PROMISED REST IN THE MIDST OF CRISIS

God gives his daughters comforting and empowering rest in the midst of crises. He gives them the needed amount of rest and comfort when they most need it.

This is the "letting-go" rest Christian women can count on from a loving Heavenly Father when they face a painful situation. They need divine intervention in order to walk through their valley, and God sends it in the form of strength, calmness, acceptance, and divine rest.

These are the times God promises *to carry us* when we can no longer walk on our own. These are the times the Holy Spirit promises *to pray* for us when pain hinders us from praying for ourselves. "In the same way, the Spirit helps us in our weakness. We do not know what we ought to pray for, but the Spirit himself intercedes for us with groans that words cannot express. And he who searches our hearts knows the mind of the Spirit, because the Spirit intercedes for the saints in accordance with God's will" (Rom. 8:26–27). These are the times we can confidently place ourselves wholly in God's hands and trust him completely in all things.

Practical Suggestions

Are you, like Deborah Cooper, facing the crisis of a loved one's deteriorating health? Are you dealing with other crises that send you crying out to God for his special help—crises such as a wayward child, an unfaithful spouse, personal illnesses, anticipated surgery, grieving a loved one's death from disease, accident, or murder? Here are some practical suggestions that may help you during your times of crisis.

⚜ Read John 15:9–15 and meditate upon its meaning. Ponder the meaning of the Father's love for you. Think of yourself as a "branch" firmly attached to God the "vine." Whenever you feel discouraged, bring to mind that beautiful, loving image.

- Spend as much time as possible in a quiet place and in prayer. Just sit and rest in God's love and presence, and let him give you needed strength.

- Pray that God will send you friends who will help you in some of the areas you most need help. When people ask whether they can help you, respond with a "yes" and allow them to minister to you during the crisis.

- If possible, spend time with friends and allow them to encourage you.

- If the situation allows, continue to worship in church services and stay close to your church, pastor, and members.

- When the crisis passes, whether it lasts a day or much longer, take the lessons you learned and become a "wounded healer" to a person going through the same or similar crisis.

- Read the "Footprints Prayer" when you need to know that God loves you and helps you in your crises.[8]

Personal Quiet Time to Rest, Study, Reflect, and Pray

1. Scriptures: Please read, study, and contemplate the following verses:

Psalm 34:17–18: "The righteous cry out,
and *the* LORD *hears them*;
he delivers them from all their troubles.
The LORD is close to the *brokenhearted*
and saves those who are *crushed in spirit*."

Psalm 55:22: "Cast your cares upon the LORD
and he will sustain you;
he will never let the righteous fall" (NIV 1984).

John 14:16: "And I will ask the Father, and he will give you another Counselor to be with you forever—the Spirit of truth . . . you know him, for he lives with you and will be in you" (NIV 1984).

John 14:20: "I am in my Father, and you are in me, and I am in you."

Jesus said in **Matthew 11:28**: "'Come to Me, all you who labor and are heavy laden, and I will give you rest'" (ESV). Jesus himself experienced *despair* in his life on Earth. By his own example, he showed women their need for rest, and how to find *biblical rest*.

Exodus 33:14, God promises: "My Presence will go with you, and *I will give you rest*."

2. Questions: Please reflect upon and respond to the following:

How does Deborah Cooper's situation and her devotion to Christ in the midst of the pain encourage you in your own crisis?

What questions might you want to ask Deborah if you could speak to her?

Consider and think about the crisis times in your own life. How did God bring you rest in your own pain and suffering?

Think about your friends who are currently suffering through a crisis. Decide on ways you can reach out to them with help and encouragement.

3. Prayer suggestions: Pray that you will know personally the rest and comfort Christ will bring you when you face a crisis in your life. Pray that you can be an encouragement to others who face crises and need help and comfort.

4. Decisions made (as a result of reading this chapter, studying suggested Scriptures, reflecting upon questions, and praying):

≈ Group Bible Study ≈

1. Read:

   Luke 22:42–44: "'Father, if you are willing, take this cup from me; yet not my will, but yours be done.' An angel from heaven appeared to him and strengthened him. And being in anguish, he prayed more earnestly, and his sweat was like drops of blood falling to the ground."

2. Respond: Please consider and respond to the following as a group:

   Describe Jesus' agonizing prayer recorded in Luke 22:42–44. What crisis did Jesus personally face? What did Jesus mean when he prayed: "Father, if you are willing, take this cup from me"? How did he close his prayer?

   What, in your opinion, do you think Luke meant when he wrote: "his [Jesus'] sweat was like drops of blood falling to the ground." Do you think Luke meant actual drops of blood or was he using a figure of speech? Why or why not?

Make a list of people in your family, neighborhood, community, and church who currently face crises. Think of ways your group can reach out and help them.

Take time with group members to pray together for the people you listed above.

3. Share: Reader will share with group what she has learned from this particular Bible study and the decisions she has made.

THE REST OF HEAVENLY ASSURANCE

In my Father's house are many rooms; if it were
not so, I would have told you. I am going there
to prepare a place for you. (John 14:2 NIV 1984)

_∂Q≥_ *God gives Christian women his permission to
rest in the promise of eternal life with him.* _∂Q≥_

often meet Christian women riddled with anxiety and living in deep
dread about the unstable and frightening conditions in the present
world. War. Violence. Unrest. Rumors of terrorist attacks and deaths.
Tornadoes. Earthquakes. And so many other catastrophes, both natural and man-made. They cannot fully enjoy their lives, their families,
their friends, or God's abundant gifts to them, because they are choked
with worry about the future. They look at the state of world affairs and
they cannot find hope or enjoy rest.

A SCARY WORLD

Yes, the world is a scary place to live. But should we, as Christian
women, allow the world's troubles to weigh so heavily on our hearts,

interrupt our joy, and eliminate our rest? Certainly not. Even when scientists tell us we are living in the "end days."

"For thousands of years, different religions have warned Earth about Armageddon and the final days. We are now living in an age where scientists are adding their voices and their evidence in support of end-of-the-world possibilities," reports ABC News.[1]

We hear a lot these days about the ancient Mayan civilization (in southern Mexico and northern Central America twenty-five hundred years ago) and their prediction that the world will end on December 21, 2012. Some doomsdayers believe it. Others say it is complete nonsense.[2]

Recently ABC News reported the findings (new theories) of scientists at the University of Washington. "The Earth has probably already peaked as a haven for plants and animals and begun its long descent into oblivion," they reported. "All good things must come to an end . . . at best we've got no more than half a billion years left," they predict. "After that, the planet will . . . [be] inhabited only by bacteria and single-celled organisms . . . [and] in time even those will vanish as the Earth is reduced to a lifeless chunk of rock, or swallowed entirely by an expanding Sun."[3]

We often hear of other ways the Earth may end. Some list extreme climate change as the greatest danger. Many believe the planet is growing warmer, that the ozone layer above our planet is deteriorating, and that melting glaciers will make water levels rise high enough to cover much of Earth's land.

Others believe plague will be the agent responsible for wiping out Earth's inhabitants, whether they come naturally as microscopic organisms or come by bioterrorism. Some people remember the sudden onslaught of the Spanish flu in 1918. That year, one soldier on a small military base in Kansas came down with a fever. Soon, more than one hundred soldiers at the Ft. Riley base fell ill with fever. The flu struck suddenly, causing many of its victims to die within hours of their first symptoms. In one year, the Spanish flu had spread about the whole world. It killed fifty million people, with five hundred thousand dead in the United States. My maternal grandmother's strong young brother died of the flu, and so did his soon-to-be bride. The flu germ literally jumped from one human to another. They still don't know why this particular virus mutated into its deadly form. Scientists say it could easily happen again. They still don't know how to prevent it. [4]

Some believe nuclear war, whether by accident or intention, will eliminate Earth. Or that our planet will be destroyed by a large asteroid in space that collides with Earth. Others think a super-volcano might erupt, or gamma rays from an exploding star might cause Earth's demise. Some scientists believe that a roaming black hole will swallow our planet and destroy us. "Imagine a black hole swallowing Earth, ending life in an instant. It's not only the stuff of pulp sci-fi novels but, scientists say, a looming possibility." Neil deGrasse Tyson, director of New York's Hayden Planetarium at the American Museum of Natural History admits, "It would be a bad day for the solar system if we got visited by a black hole." In our vast galaxy "there are billions upon billions of stars, each of which is at a different point in its life cycle. Citing the law of averages, some scientists believe at least one star dies every day," scientists report. "And in death, stars occasionally give birth to black holes; when a massive celestial body's core collapses, it creates an immense gravitational pull not unlike an invisible cosmic vacuum cleaner. As it moves, it sucks in all matter in its way—not even light can escape."[5]

Scientists have also long warned us about super-intelligent machines that we humans have invented and have learned to depend upon. Some believe that within decades these computerized thinking machines might become smarter than the human brain and make the decision to destroy humanity and take over Earth. "When humanity builds artificial brains millions or billions of times larger than human brains, with intelligence to match, what will that mean for us?" asks

Bill Hibbard from the University of Wisconsin–Madison. He predicts that: "Super-intelligent machines will be able to maintain social relationships with much larger groups of people, which will define their consciousness." He continues, "In his article, *Why the Future Doesn't Need Us*, Bill Joy advocated banning intelligent machines (which he called robots), genetic engineering and nanotechnology. These are all dangerous because they can self-replicate and thus get out of human control."[6]

These predictions of Earth's destruction may terrify the planet's people, but Christians need not worry about an out-of-control demolition of Earth. Why? Because the world and the entire universe rests in God's hands. He is in perfect and complete control.

Women who have put their faith and life in Christ Jesus are no longer "of this world." We don't belong here. In John 15:18–19, Jesus tells us: "If the world hates you, keep in mind that it hated me first. If you belonged to the world, it would love you as its own. As it is, *you do not belong to the world*, but I have chosen you out of the world." We live here temporarily, and, during that brief time, we enjoy God's good gifts and share the good news of salvation with others.

Our good friend Dr. Piper writes, "Whatever we possess, we enjoy for a little while, and then we are gone and it belongs to someone else. But what we possess in Christ—our salvation—is forever. 'Life in Christ is eternal—it will never pass away. Surely, God is most glorified in us when we are most satisfied in Him.'"[7]

Jesus told his friend Martha this truth after Lazarus died: "I am the resurrection and the life. He who believes in me will live, even though he dies; and whoever lives and believes in me will never die" (John 11:25–26 NIV 1984).

Jesus also assures his disciples that when our time comes to leave this earth body, we will be with him. "In my Father's house are many rooms; if it were not so, I would have told you. I am going there to prepare a place for you. And if I go and prepare a place for you, I will come back and take you to be with me that you also may be where I am" (John 14:2–3 NIV 1984).

Your place and my place, as Christ-believers, are prepared and waiting for us. God promises us this permanent eternal home with him. In that truth, I find great rest. If I had no idea where I would go when I die, I could find no joy or rest during my brief years on Earth. I would fear every report on the end of the world. I would be afraid to walk across the street or drive a car. Death would be a thought and fear that would never leave my mind. How can a nonbeliever sleep at night not knowing of her destination if she fails to wake up the next morning? I do not know. I take great hope and receive great rest in Scripture's promise to me found in John 3:16: "For God so loved the world that he gave his one and only Son, that *whoever believes in him shall not perish but have eternal life*." I believe Scripture when John 14:6 promises me: "I am the way and the truth and the life. No one comes to the Father except through me."

When I was a young girl, my family and I lived in Atlanta, Georgia. Every summer, my mother drove me to the Atlanta bus station and put me on the bus to Rossville, Georgia, a city near Chattanooga. I never felt afraid of traveling alone. I knew that the moment the bus stopped in Rossville, my grandparents would meet me at the bus door and take me to their home. I could rest and enjoy the bus ride because I knew Mama and Papa would be waiting for me when I arrived.

I believe leaving earth for heaven will be the same. God himself will be at our death's door to meet us and welcome us home. This knowledge, confirmed by Scripture, gives women the ultimate rest. They can choose then to live freely, happily, and worry free because they know where they are going when they depart from their physical life. There is ultimate peace and rest and security when a Christian woman isn't afraid of death and when she knows for sure her final destiny, her true home.

I have long admired the person and the work of Billy Graham. My grandfather, George M. Williams, heard the young Billy Graham preach in Florida before he became well known. "That young man will go far!" he told everybody when he returned home to Chattanooga. I've had the joy of telling this story to two of Graham's daughters and a grandson. In his new book *Nearing Home*, the Reverend Graham states:

> Heaven is our home—our final home—our ultimate place of complete peace and security and joy forever. Here our homes are imperfect, even at best . . . but this isn't true of Heaven. When we belong to Christ, we know that when we die we finally will be at peace—for we will be home. Paul's words to the Christians in Corinth apply to us as well: "As long as we are at home in the body we are away from the Lord . . . [but we] would prefer to be away from the body and at home with the Lord" (2 Cor. 5:6, 8). Heaven is our hope, Heaven is our future, and Heaven is our home![8]

In that fact, we can find the ultimate rest!

Practical Suggestions

How do you and I, as Christian women, keep a Christ-centered perspective throughout our daily lives, resting in the "bigger picture" of life with eternity as our reward and future home with our Lord?

- ⸮ Memorize this verse and repeat it to yourself often: "In my Father's house are many rooms; if it were not so, I would have told you. I am going there to prepare a place for you. And if I go and prepare a place for you, I will come back and take you to be with me that you also may be where I am" (John 14:2–3 NIV 1984). Believe it, trust it, and live it!

- ⸮ Reach out to hurting others in this world, and help them as best you can, but always remember that earth-life is temporary, not eternal. Tell others that Jesus is "the way and the truth and the life. No one comes to the Father except through me" (John 14:6).

- ☙ Teach your children the meaning of John 3:16: "For God so loved the world that he gave his one and only Son, that *whoever believes in him shall not perish but have eternal life.*"

- ☙ Stay in close touch with God through prayer. Don't let the everyday world's concern drag you down. Escape often to your prayer place and rest in your Father's love and peace.

- ☙ Ask God for guidance as you make important decisions. Ask him to help you make these decisions from the perspective of eternity.

- ☙ Pray for the world, but with the understanding that you are in Christ and you no longer belong to the world. Invest yourself in eternal things, not in the temporary things of life.

- ☙ When you feel a longing for a desire you can't seem to satisfy here on earth, read this statement by C. S. Lewis in his book *Mere Christianity*: "If I find in myself a desire which no experience in this world can satisfy, the most probable explanation is that I was made for another world."[9]

Personal Quiet Time to Rest, Study, Reflect, and Pray

1. Scriptures: Please read, study, and contemplate the following verses:

John 3:16: "For God so loved the world that he gave his one and only Son, that *whoever believes in him shall not perish but have eternal life.*"

John 15:18–19: "If the world hates you, keep in mind that it hated me first. If you belonged to the world, it would love you as its own. As it is, *you do not belong to the world*, but I have chosen you out of the world."

2. Questions: Please reflect upon and respond to the following:

   What is your greatest fear and why?

   What kind of assurance does John 3:16 give you about life after physical death?

   What is meant by "eternal life" in John 3:16?

   What does this Scripture passage mean to you: *"you do not belong to the world*, but I have chosen you out of the world" (John 15:19)?

   Does God's assurance of your place in heaven give you rest? If so, how does this fact influence your life today?

3. Prayer suggestions: Thank God that "He so loved the world that he gave his one and only Son, that *whoever believes in him shall not perish but have eternal life.*"

   If you haven't yet made that decision to believe and commit your life to Christ alone, ask God to help you make that decision right now.

4. Decisions made (as a result of reading this chapter, studying suggested Scriptures, reflecting upon questions, and praying):

∞ Group Bible Study ∞

1. Read:

   John 14:6: "I am the way and the truth and the life. No one comes to the Father except through me."

   Psalm 23:6: "Surely goodness and love will follow me
   all the days of my life,
   and I will dwell in the house of the LORD
   forever."

   John 11:25:"I am the resurrection and the life. He who believes in me will live, even though he dies; and whoever lives and believes in me will never die" (NIV 1984).

   John 14:2–3: "In my Father's house are many rooms; if it were not so, I would have told you. I am going there to prepare a place for you. And if I go and prepare a place for you, I will come back and take you to be with me that you also may be where I am" (NIV 1984).

   Romans 6:23: "For the wages of sin is death, but the gift of God is eternal life in Christ Jesus our Lord."

2. Respond: Please consider and respond to the following as a group:

   After reading the Scripture verses above, what do you believe about Jesus, Heaven, and the assurance of salvation in Christ?

   What do you think Heaven will consist of? Describe how Heaven might look.

What has God done, through Jesus Christ, to reconcile the world to him? How can we best share that good news with a world that needs to hear it?

3. Share: Reader will share with group what she has learned from this particular Bible Study and the decisions she has made.

ENDNOTES

INTRODUCTION

1   John Eldredge, *Wild at Heart* (Nashville, TN: Thomas Nelson, 2001), 17.

2   Anne Morrow Lindberg, *Wisdom from Gift from the Sea* (White Plains, NY: Peter Pauper, 2002).

3   http://stress.about.com/od/stresshealth/a/cortisol.htm. Accessed: June 20, 2012

4   http://www.five-minutestressrelief.com/Stress_Statistics.html, accessed September 18, 2010.

5   George Barna, http://www.baptiststandard.com/2000/4_3/pages/women.html, accessed June 28, 2005.

6   Ibid.

CHAPTER 1

1   Henri J. M. Nouwen, *Making All Things New* (New York: Phoenix Press; Walker and Company, 1981), 23.

2   Lindberg, *Wisdom*.

3   "Americans Just Want a Good Night of Sleep," http://www.barna.org/barna-update/article/13-culture/145-americans-just-want-a-good-night-of-sleep, accessed October 16, 2006.

4   "Stages of Sleep: REM and Non-REM Sleep," *WebMD*, http://www.webmd.com/sleep-disorders/excessive-sleepiness-10/sleep-101?page=2, accessed September 21, 2010.

5   "The Sweet Science of Dozing", *MedicineNet.com*, http://www.medicinenet.com/script/main/art.asp?articlekey=50785, accessed May 3, 2012.

6   Ibid.

7   Daniel K. Hall-Flavin, "What's the difference between normal stress and an adjustment disorder?" *Mayo Clinic Health Information*, http://www.mayoclinic.com/health/adjustment-disorder/AN01768, accessed September 29, 2010.

8   "Stress symptoms: Effects on your body, feelings and behavior," *Mayo Clinic Health Information*, http://www.mayoclinic.com/health/stress-symptoms/SR00008_D, accessed September 29, 2010.

9   Paul Brand and Philip Yancey, *In His Image* (Grand Rapids, MI: Zondervan, 1984), 255.

10 Karl Menninger, *Whatever Became of Sin?* (New York: Hawthorn Books, 1973), 91.

11 Stacy Wiebe, "Tips for Women Who Juggle Too Much," *Women Today*, www.womentodaymagazine.com/career/busyness.html, accessed July 15, 2005.

12 Richard J. Foster and Emilie Griffin, *Spiritual Classics* (San Francisco, CA: HarperSanFrancisco, 2000), 160.

13 "Pet Health Pictures Slideshow: 27 Ways Pets Can Improve Your Health," *MedicineNet*, http://www.medicinenet.com/script/main/art.asp?articlekey=105279, accessed September 21, 2010.

14 Polly Leider, "When Women's Fatigue Signals Danger," *CBSNews*, Jan. 30, 2006, http://www.cbsnews.com/stories/2006/01/30/earlyshow/health/main1259346.shtml?tag=contentMain;contentBody, accessed: Sept. 19, 2010.

CHAPTER 2

1   Wayne E. Oates, *Managing Your Stress* (Indianapolis, IN: Bierce, 1983), 27.

2   "Stress and the Workplace," *LifePositive*, http://www.lifepositive.com/mind/psychology/stress/stress-at-work.asp, accessed: Oct. 3, 2010.

3   NIOSH, "Women's Safety and Health Issues at Work Fact Sheet," http://www.cdc.gov/niosh/docs/2001–123/, accessed October 3, 2010.

4   Catherine Rampell, "As Layoffs Surge, Women May Pass Men in Job Force," *New York Times*, February 5, 2009, http://www.nytimes.com/2009/02/06/business/06women.html?_r=2&pagewanted=all, accessed October 3, 2010.

5   NIOSH, "Women's Safety and Health Issues at Work."

6   Ibid.

7   Ibid.

8   Natalie J. Jordet and Erica Lumiere, "Is Job Stress Making You Sick?" *Marie Claire*, June 1, 2000, http://www.marieclaire.com/career-money/jobs/articles/job-stress, accessed October 3, 2010.

9   "Stress and the Workplace," *LifePositive*.

10 Amy Joyce, "Household Chores Conform to Stereotype: In the Work-Family Balancing Act, Women Still Do Most of the Juggling,"

Washington Post, September 19, 2004, F05, http://www.washingtonpost.
com/wp-dyn/articles/A30812-2004Sep18.html, accessed October 3, 2010.

11 Rampell, "As Layoffs Surge."

12 Robert McKelvie, "Fairness in Allocating Household Chores,"
Marriage @ Suite101, Aug 2, 2010, http://www.suite101.com/content/
fairness-in-allocating-household-chores-a268994, accessed October 4,
2010.

13 Wiebe, "Tips for Women Who Juggle Too Much."

14 Emilie Barnes, *The Spirit of Loveliness* (Eugene, OR: Harvest
House, 1992), 90.

15 H. Norman Wright, *Simplify Your Life*, 1998, 39. Quoted in Gary
Petty, "Are You Missing Out on A Blessing From God?" *The Good News*
(Carol Stream, IL: Tyndale House Publishers, 1998) http://www.
gnmagazine.org/issues/gn31/blessing.htm, accessed November 6, 2010.

16 "Think Your Are Multitasking? Think Again," *npr*, http://www.
npr.org/templates/story/story.php?storyId=95256794

17 Menninger, *Whatever Became of Sin?*, 91.

18 "Nurture Mental, Emotional, and Physical Health during Job
Search," *WomensJobList*, http://www.womensjoblist.com/blog/
414-Nurture-Mental,-Emotional,-and-Physical-Health-During-Job-
Search.html, accessed November 6, 2010.

19 Larry Burkett, *Women Leaving the Workplace* (Chicago: Moody
Press, 1995), 14.

20 McKelvie, "Fairness in Allocating Household Chores."

CHAPTER 3

1 Max Anders, *Holman New Testament Commentary on Galatians,
Ephesians, Philippians, Colossians* (Nashville, TN: Holman Reference,
1999), 266.

2 Stephen D. Eyre, *Drawing Close to God* (Downers Grove, IL:
InterVarsity Press, 1995), title page.

3 http://encyclopedia2.thefreedictionary.com/Christ+the+
Redeemer+of+the+Andes. Accessed: June 20, 2012

4 Charles H. Spurgeon, "Spiritual Peace," February 19, 1860, http://
www.biblebb.com/files/spurgeon/0300.htm, accessed December 15, 2011.

CHAPTER 4

1 Quoted in Gary and Barbara Rosberg, *The Five Love Needs of Men and Women* (Wheaton, IL: Tyndale, 2000), 200.

2 Quoted in Stephen D. Eyre, *Drawing Close to God: The Essentials of a Dynamic Quiet Time* (Downers Grove, IL: InterVarsity Press, 1995), n.p. Quoted from Logos Bible Software 4.

3 Charles H. Spurgeon, *Morning and Evening: Daily Readings.* Complete and unabridged; New modern edition (Peabody, MA: Hendrickson, 2006). Quoted in Morning, October 12, "I will meditate in thy precepts." Logos Bible Software 4.

CHAPTER 5

1 "Inspirational Quotes about Humility," *Values.com*, http://www.values.com/inspirational-quotes/value/27-Humility, accessed February 11, 2012.

2 "Humility Quotes," *Finest Quotes*, http://www.finestquotes.com/select_quote-category-Humility-page-0.htm, accessed February 11, 2012.

3 Quoted in Denise George, *Learning to Forgive Those Who Hurt You* (Corona, CA: Sine Qua Non, 2011), 51.

4 Alistair Begg, *The Hand of God* (Chicago: Moody, 1999), 161.

5 Quoted in John MacArthur, *In the Freedom and Power of Forgiveness*, quoted in Robert Jeffress, *When Forgiveness Doesn't Make Sense* (Colorado Springs: WaterBrook, 2000), 55.

6 Quoted in George, *Learning to Forgive*, 10.

CHAPTER 7

1 G. Sweeting, *Moody Monthly*, May, 1988, 95. http://www.innovationtools.com/Articles/ArticleDetails.asp?a=477, accessed May 1, 2012 5/1/12; Andy Andrews, "Acres of Diamonds," *Face Today*, http://www.warrenmartin.com/facetoday-discussion/2010/6/20/ft-62110-acres-of-diamonds.html, accessed February 17, 2012.

2 Charles Spurgeon, "Charles Spurgeon on Contentment,"*oChristian.com*, http://christian-quotes.ochristian.com/christian-quotes_ochristian.cgi?find=Christian-quotes-by-Charles+Spurgeon-on-Contentment, accessed February 17, 2012.

3 Charles H. Spurgeon, "Contentment: A Sermon," March 25, 1860, *The Spurgeon Archive*, http://www.spurgeon.org/sermons/0320.htm, accessed February 17, 2012.

4 "Mamertine Prison, Rome," *Sacred Destinations*, http://www. sacred-destinations.com/italy/rome-mamertine-prison, accessed April 8, 2010.

5 Augustine, "Augustine on Contentment,"*oChristian.com*, http:// christian-quotes.ochristian.com/christian-quotes_ochristian.cgi? find=Christian-quotes-by-Augustine-on-Contentment, accessed February 17, 2012.

6 John Piper, *God's Passion for His Glory* (Wheaton, IL: Crossway), 41.

7 Warren Wiersbe, "Warren Wiersbe on Contentment," *oChristian. com*, http://christian-quotes.ochristian.com/christian-quotes_ ochristian.cgi?find=Christian-quotes-by-Warren+Wiersbe-on-Contentment, accessed February 17, 2012.

8 Elisabeth Elliot and Lisa Barry, "Contentment: One Prisoner's Story," *Back to the Bible*, http://www.backtothebible.org/index.php/ Gateway-to-Joy/Contentment-One-Prisoner-s-Story.html, accessed February 17, 2012.

9 A. W. Pink, "A. W. Pink on Contentment," *oChristian.com*, http:// christian-quotes.ochristian.com/christian-quotes_ochristian.cgi?find- =Christian-quotes-by-A.W.+Pink-on-Contentment, accessed February 17, 2012.

10 http://www.brainyquote.com/quotes/authors/h/helen_keller.html, Accessed: 5/1/12, accessed May 1, 2012.

11 "Helen Keller Home," http://www.helenkellerbirthplace.org/ helenkellerhome/helen_keller_birthplace2_home.htm, accessed February 18, 2012.

12 Helen Keller, "Helen Keller on Contentment," *oChristian.com*, http://christian-quotes.ochristian.com/christian-quotes_ochristian. cgi?find=Christian-quotes-by-Helen+Keller-on-Contentment, accessed February 17, 2012.

13 "It Is Well with My Soul: The Song and the Story," *Afterhours Inspirational Stories*, http://www.inspirationalstories.com/it-is-well-with-my-soul-the-song-and-the-story/, accessed February 17, 2012.

14 David Jeremiah, "First-Person: Contentment: When Enough Is Enough," *Baptist Press*, Nov 17, 2006, http://www.bpnews.net/bpnews.asp?id=24421, accessed February 17, 2012.

15 "Sermon Illustrations: Contentment," *HotSermons*, http://hotsermons.com/sermon-illustrations/sermon-illustrations-contentment.html, accessed February 17, 2012.

16 J. I. Packer, "J. I. Packer on Contentment," *oChristian.com*, http://christian-quotes.ochristian.com/christian-quotes_ochristian.cgi?find=Christian-quotes-by-J.I.+Packer-on-Contentment, accessed February 17, 2012.

CHAPTER 8

1 Annie Dillard, *Pilgrim at Tinker Creek*, http://www.goodreads.com/author/quotes/5209.Annie_Dillard, accessed May 1, 2012.

CHAPTER 9

1 U.S. Department of Labor, Bureau of Labor Statistics. *Women in the Labor Force: A Databook*. September 2008, http://www.bls.gov/cps/wlf-databook2008.htm, accessed February 18, 2012.

2 Statistics from Jennifer Wolf, "Single Parent Statistics," *About.com*, http://singleparents.about.com/od/legalissues/p/portrait.htm, accessed February 18, 2010.

3 "Mothers by the Numbers," *infoplease*, http://www.infoplease.com/spot/momcensus1.html, accessed February 18, 2012. In 2002, the United Stated Census determined that three out of every ten children being raised in America are living in single-parent homes. Unfortunately, the number of single-parent homes is growing. In addition to divorce, you have to remember that many people are choosing to have children without a partner. Therefore, with our society being much more accepting of the non-traditional home, the numbers are staggering. Renee Dietz, "Just How Many Single Parents Are There?" *families.com*, http://single-parenting.families.com/blog/just-how-many-single-parents-are-there, accessed February 18, 2012.

4 "Grandparents Raising Grandchildren,"*Grandparenting.org*, http://www.grandparenting.org/Grandparents_Raising_Grandchildren.htm, accessed February 19, 2012.

5 "Kids Count Datacenter," *The Annie E. Casey Foundation*, http://
datacenter.kidscount.org/data/acrossstates/Rankings.aspx?ind=102,
accessed February 18, 2012.

6 Amber Keefer, "The Role of Motherhood," *Livestrong*, http://www.
livestrong.com/article/79456-role-motherhood/#ixzz1mlTv7Z1y, accessed
February 18, 2012.

7 Ibid.

8 "Parenting: Being supermom stressing you out?" *American
Psychological Association*, http://www.apa.org/helpcenter/supermom.aspx,
accessed February 18, 2012.

9 Ibid.

10 Ibid.

11 "National Survey of Mothers With Kids Under Six Finds . . ."
PRNewswire, August 23, 2011, http://www.prnewswire.com/news-
releases/national-survey-of-mothers-with-kids-under-six-finds-128242408.
html, accessed February 17, 2012.

12 "Selected Caregiver Statistics," *Family Caregiver Alliance*, http://
www.caregiver.org/caregiver/jsp/content_node.jsp?nodeid=439, accessed
February 18, 2012.

13 Dessina King quoted in "Caretakers Syndrome: Neglecting Your
Needs When Caring for Another," *Urban Housecall*, http://www.
urbanhousecallmagazine.com/caretakers-syndrome-neglecting-
your-needs-when-caring-for-another/, accessed February 19, 2012.

14 "Selected Caregiver Statistics," *Family Caregiver Alliance*.

15 Names have been changed to protect privacy.

16 Ibid.

17 "Parenting," *APA*.

CHAPTER 10

1 "Roman Timeline 1st Century AD," *UNRV History*, http://www.
unrv.com/empire/timeline-of-first-century.php, accessed February 20,
2012.

2 Dictionary of Bible Themes, Logos Edition #4470. Martin H.
Manser, *Dictionary of Bible Themes: The Accessible and Comprehensive Tool
for Topical Studies* (London, 1999.)

Chapter 12

1 "The Story Behind 'The Praying Hands,'" *Afterhours Inspirational Stories*, April 17, 2011, http://www.inspirationalstories.com/the-story-behind-the-praying-hands/, accessed February 17, 2012.

2 Gale Berkowitz, "UCLA Study on Friendship Among Women: An Alternative to Fight or Flight," *Chronic Neuroimmune Diseases*, http://www.anapsid.org/cnd/gender/tendfend.html, accessed February 21, 2012.

3 Ibid.

4 Ibid.

5 Stephanie Wagle, "Making and Keeping Friends as an Adult," *Parents*, http://www.parents.com/parenting/relationships/friendship/making-and-keeping-friends-as-an-adult/, accessed February 21, 2012.

6 Bridget Hughes, "The Healing Power of Friendship," *CBS Interactive Business Network Resource Library*, May 2005, http://findarticles.com/p/articles/mi_go2717/is_147/ai_n32037755/, accessed February 21, 2012.

7 Jennifer Gerics, "Women and Friendship: Female Bonds Have Both Psychological and Physical Health Benefits, *"Women's Health @ Suite 101*, August 12, 2008, http://jennifergerics.suite101.com/women_and_friendship-a64040, accessed February 21, 2012.

8 Ibid.

9 Martha Edwards, "Women and Friendships: Why We Are Falling Behind in Keeping Up Our Social Lives," *Huffington Post*, September 28, 2011, http://www.huffingtonpost.ca/2011/09/26/women-friends_n_982245.html, accessed February 21, 2012.

10 Melissa Healy, "Our Innate Need for Friendship," *LA Times*, May 9, 2005, http://articles.latimes.com/2005/may/09/health/he-friends9, accessed February 21, 2012.

11 Ibid.

Chapter 13

1 "Footprints Prayer," http://prayer-and-prayers.info/favorite-prayers/footprints-prayer.htm, accessed February 22, 2012.

2 David B. Hall, "Across the Nations: 66 of the World's Worst Disasters," http://across.co.nz/WorldsWorstDisasters.html, accessed February 22, 2012.

3 "Chernobyl Accident 1986," *World Nuclear Association*, updated March 2012, http://www.world-nuclear.org/info/chernobyl/inf07.html, accessed February 22, 2012.

4 "First World War Casualties," *History Learning Site*, http://www. historylearningsite.co.uk/FWWcasualties.htm, accessed February 22, 2012.

5 "Estimated War Dead: World War II," *warchronicle.com*, http:// warchronicle.com/numbers/WWII/deaths.htm, accessed February 22, 2012.

6 Boot Camp for Christian Writers: These writing-to-publish seminars are taught by Denise George and Carolyn Tomlin, and are part of Beeson Divinity School's Lay Academy of Theology program.

7 "Progressive supranuclear palsy," *Mayo Clinic*, http://www. mayoclinic.com/health/progressive-supranuclear-palsy/DS00909, accessed February 22, 2012.

8 You can find the poem at this website: http://prayer-and-prayers. info/favorite-prayers/footprints-prayer.htm.

CHAPTER 14

1 "Last Days on Earth,"*20/20*, http://abcnews.go.com/2020/story?id=2319986#.T0Z7RWCNrac, accessed February 23, 2012.

2 Daniel Schwartz, "Did the Maya Predict the World Would End in 2012?"*CBCNews*, http://www.cbc.ca/news/world/story/2012/01/05/f-2012-maya-calendar.html, accessed February 23, 2012.

3 Lee Dye, "When Will the World End? New Theory Emerges," *ABCNews*, http://abcnews.go.com/Technology/story?id=97756 &page=1#.T0Zn9mCNrac, accessed February 22, 2012.

4 Jennifer Rosenberg, "1918 Spanish Flu Pandemic," *About.com*, http://history1900s.about.com/od/1910s/p/spanishflu.htm, accessed February 17, 2012.

5 "Black Holes: The Deadliest Force in the Universe," *20/20*, Aug. 28, 2006, http://abcnews.go.com/2020/Science/story?id=2365372&page=1#. T0Zzh2CNrac, accessed February 23, 2012.

6 Bill Hibbard, "Super-Intelligent Machines," November 13, 2001, http://www.ssec.wisc.edu/~billh/visfiles.html, accessed February 23, 2012.

7   John Piper, "John Piper on Contentment," *oChristian.com*, http://
christian-quotes.ochristian.com/christian-quotes_ochristian.cgi?
find=Christian-quotes-by-John+Piper-on-Contentment, accessed
February 17, 2012.

8   Billy Graham, *Nearing Home: Life, Faith, And Finishing Well*
(Nashville, TN: Thomas Nelson, 2011), 178, 179.

9   C. S. Lewis, *Mere Christianity* (New York: HarperCollins, 1952),
136.